kindness for conflict

A Guide to Separation & Divorce

Tosh Brittan

Founder of Divorce Goddess

Kindness for Conflict: A Guide to Separation & Divorce

© Tosh Brittan Coaching, 2023

For permission requests, email hello@divorcegoddess.com

Tosh Brittan Coaching.

www.divorcegoddess.com

Edited by Kerry Laundon and Rachael Chilvers

Book production by Shamash Alidina

Author photography by Vicki Knights Photography

Table of Contents

Endorsements

"We recommend that all going through a divorce or separation read this book. It shares many useful practical tips and has been written with warmth, sincerity, and a genuine desire to help" Rebecca Giraud and Bob Greig. Co-directors of OnlyMums & Dads CIC. Co-editors of (Almost) Anything but Family Court (Bath Publishing).

"A 'must-read' for anyone thinking about or going through divorce or separation. This practical and inspirational book will guide you with useful tools in what is often a very painful and challenging time. Congratulations Tosh on an empowering and potentially life-changing book for many." Sue Stone, Author, Speaker & Transformational Leader. www.suestone.com

"Kindness for Conflict offers separating couples and families hope that there is a better way, and gives them tips to use along the way. It looks at how changing a few small things, and remembering what you can (and cannot) control, can make big differences and lead to positive outcomes. I thoroughly recommend this book, which is brimming with positivity. You CAN have a kinder separation!" Rebecca Hawkins, Family Solutions, Specialist in non-court options for families

"I love that you shared your divorce intention, very powerful. This book is empowering, inspiring and practical. When you feel that you have no control, it's the perfect place to turn to understand the true power you hold within." Ceri Griffiths FPFS CeMap BSC Hons Chartered Financial Planner, Willow Brook Lifestyle Financial Planning

"An exceptional approach to separation and divorce. Kindness for Conflict provides you with useful tools and the shift in mindset you need to not only get through but embrace the challenge divorce presents. It ensures you take every opportunity to do it in the kindest way possible, for everyone, including you and is a "must read" for any separating or divorcing couple." Lottie Kent, Award Winning Chartered Financial Planner & Resolution Accredited Divorce Specialist

"Kindness is not often a word associated with divorce, but this book offers anyone going through a separation the hope that it is possible. It is a shining light there to guide separating couples. It is jam packed with lots of tips to show that small changes really can make a big difference. The book is enlightening, empowering, and a real must read for anyone starting out on their divorce journey. It's a timely reminder that you have the power to decide what your divorce will look like." - Liza Gattrell, Family Lawyer

Dedication

This book is dedicated to my children, Bella and Felix, and their beautiful hearts.

It is for my Ex-husband for being part of this kindness journey.

It is also for those who I love and who love me, those who have been on this journey with me, and those I've met on the way.

Preface

Welcome to *Kindness for Conflict: A Guide to Separation & Divorce*. This book is in your hands for a reason. Whether you picked it up because you're embarking on a separation journey, the cheery yellow cover popped out at you, or something inside you struck a chord and you felt hopeful after reading the title, I trust with all my heart that it helps you get through this difficult and painful time.

Whatever spoke to you, trust it. For the most part, we live in a world where we stay with what we know and are comfortable with, so we've lost much of the ability to believe and trust in ourselves to do more. We often miss those moments of clarity that appear when we're more present in our lives, and these in turn lead us to feeling more confident so we can make wiser, calmer and kinder decisions, no matter what conflict we're dealing with in life.

Society has a big part to play in how divorce is viewed; more often than not it is with looks of pity, words of sadness and wide-ranging judgements centred around the view that all divorces are hell-bound. The culture of failure and shame around divorce defines the process and supports this viewpoint. With almost half of married couples divorcing, divorce deserves a better rap.

A certain air descends on folk when the word 'divorce' is mentioned. An ex-judge once remarked, "Divorce is the scourge of society." Yet with so many couples getting a divorce, we need to find a way to encourage a kinder process to reduce conflict and change the face of this sad and challenging experience.

Getting a divorce needs to be validated and respected as a badge of honour for coming through the painful and crazily uncertain days. Finding the strength to get up every day can be exhausting.

I grew up as a child of divorced parents. What I remember, amongst the fights, fears of the 'what ifs' and ensuing logistics, is that the judge told my parents, "I have never known such a friendly divorce." This was in the early '80s, when divorce was relatively rare. Buoyed up by these kind words, they walked out of the courtroom arm in arm. Although their 'friendly divorce' didn't last as long as we all hoped, I believe that glimmer of possibility stayed with me long into my life and for my future divorce for a reason. Funny the stuff that sticks, right?

Why am I telling you this? Shortly after my Ex and I split, a couple of corporate lawyer friends told me I had to take my Ex to court and take him for all we had (left), and all I could feel was a rock in my belly and a sick feeling of fear at the thought. It got me thinking – did I really want to feel my guts twisted up like this for the next however many months, or possibly years? I thought, "No, I can do this better," and I decided to see my divorce as an experiment in kindness. With every stage, I was going to be kind, no matter what was happening, being said or what I thought my Ex was thinking, and see what would happen.

I remember the first few people we told about our divorce were so sad, disappointed, disorientated and unprepared – where did this leave them? Seeing the looks on our loved ones' faces encouraged me further to make a promise to myself that, no matter what was going to happen to my Ex and I, damage limitation was now paramount. I was going to make damn sure we were going to have as kind a divorce as possible.

This book is not an attempt to shame others who are in the middle of a sh*tstorm and stuck in a world of pain. It is a guide to help people through thinking about or going through separation and divorce. I'm not saying divorce is great, happy-clappy or easy – hell no – but I believe it is time to see and do divorce differently.

If you're ready to be part of a growing movement to change the face of divorce by adding compassion and kindness to the process, I am happy you're here. Reading this book, you will not only be growing your strength over fear muscles, but also committing to yourself by putting time into this new way of thinking, feeling and acting. Accepting that there will be good days when you can let stuff go, and bad days when you can't. You will step into your fears, bust through them and feel more empowered as a result.

Divorcees aren't the weak ones that couldn't stay the course of a marriage or relationship; they are strong and resilient, and their future is unavoidably shaped by what happens around and within this life-changing event. How you want your future to look is up to you. Kindness can be your superpower.

This book aims to support you, empower you and help you grow, release your inner brave and most courageous parts, and live through your separation and divorce with kindness, compassion and less conflict. Put simply, this book is about your divorce being about YOU and not your Ex. I want for you to get through your separation knowing you did your best, and that is enough.

Introduction

divorce

/dɪˈvɔːs/

Noun: The legal dissolution of a marriage by a court or other competent body.

Synonyms: dissolution, annulment, official separation, judicial separation, separation, disunion, breakup, split, split-up, severance, rupture, breach, parting, khula, talaq

Opposite: marriage

With all this negativity, no wonder divorce feels like the dumpster of shame!

I'm going to be honest with you. I still get triggered by my divorce and my Ex. I'm not always a 'Divorce Goddess'. With all my years of experience and training in coaching and healing, I am still human and one thing I know is that life is one continuous learning journey for us all. Nope, I am not perfect, nor have I ever hoped I could be – but I had hope that I'd find perfection in the acceptance of my imperfection. During my divorce, I committed wholeheartedly and courageously (it took ALL my guts) to base every decision on kindness and positivity as opposed to conflict, and in the bleakest of moments this gave me a CHOICE.

Yes, I still have those painful, sad and gut-kicking thoughts that hurt me when I least expect it – of not having years of memories to share with our grandchildren in that 'married forever' way, with comfy armchairs to do the crossword in and family photos on the mantlepiece of us all smiling together.

Seeing happily married friends together can still leave me with a deep sadness that I try to replace with unbridled enthusiasm for them staying together through thick and thin, despite the ups and downs. I've had therapy to unblock and unlock, welcome in and release fear and negativity, and be open and commit to love again. I have bought courses that promised personal heartbreak transformation in eight weeks. What I know now is this: we will do pretty much anything to access that magic panacea that will take us to post-divorce nirvana without the work.

"When I grow up, I wish with all my heart to be a divorcee," said no one, ever!

I certainly didn't, and I know my Ex didn't, and I'm pretty damn sure you didn't have that on your bucket list either. And yet somehow divorce is happening to almost half of the population… and we never thought it would happen to us?

A 'good' divorce sounds like a total contradiction, but why does it have to be any other way? It won't necessarily be without its painful moments, and like anything in life you have to put the work in to get there. It takes courage, kindness and a willingness to think outside of the proverbial war – where you're standing on the battlefield and fighting in and out of court. Learning to do anything new, like walking, riding a bike or learning another language, takes practice, time and, yes, we fall down and it can be hard.

But why is a kind divorce so difficult to grasp? Does it stray so far away from our social norms that it feels unobtainable, impossible or ridiculous (yep, people have laughed at me)? Does it go against everything we've been conditioned to believe about the divorce process? Instead of settling for this unhelpful understanding of what divorce looks like, why not use this opportunity to upgrade yourself from the 'divorce-centric', angry, bitter and resentful person that you don't want to be, and mitigate the damage caused by conflict and high emotions to yourself and your kids? Having a kinder divorce is all about YOU believing YOU CAN and showing up for yourself each day, no matter what your Ex is up to, so you live in alignment with your values. *You* are who you're going to live with for the rest of your life, not your Ex, so take a moment to think to yourself – who would I rather live with: someone who was kind, dignified and believed in a better way of doing their divorce, or someone who chose not to? Like anything good in life, the alternative path is never easy, but the rewards are so worth it.

Divorce: The Most Human of Experiences

I have met many clients and divorcees who never thought on the day of "I do" that they would find themselves later divorcing. With nearly 50% of marriages ending in divorce, think about how many people are looking at their Decree Nisi and trying to fathom out how they got there!

Divorce is a harsh reality of modern life. It is not, as some judge, a badge of failure or the easy option when things start going pear-shaped. Divorce is not a walk in the park – it's a trek beyond Base Camp and you don't get no Sherpas! It is, after a death, the hardest and most painful life event we go through – that's why it's called a living grief, because it never leaves you, especially if you have children.

There are generations that have stayed stuck in a difficult marriage for the children, financial reasons or because they were more scared of the consequences of leaving than of staying. Maybe your parents were those people? Perhaps as a child or teenager you felt deep down inside you that something didn't sit right about the unhappiness or lack of authenticity in their relationship. You may not have seen much love, but many arguments and a sweeping under the carpet of much ado about EVERYTHING. Our parents' marriage/relationship can teach us how to love, and if this experience doesn't come from a place of kindness, trust and respect, how might this impact us? By the time my dear parents split, the relief was palpable. They taught me much about how to be and how not to be married and divorced, but also about love and endings. But they, like so many others, showed me that they were human, that humans make mistakes, and that although we may err from righteous marital paths, there can be hope at the end of the tunnel.

The Emotional Whirlwind of Divorce

Society is not a fan of divorce. Divorce threatens the status quo and the comfort of others but most of all ourselves, rocked by emotions such as grief and sadness, guilt and fear. We are societally programmed to go into a divorce with conflict, as angry fighters rather than calm negotiators. To tear apart all that we have built, rather than rebuild something better with any kindness we have left. We are directed to be mistrustful and angry, fearful and powerless, but it doesn't have to be this way. You can choose how you as an individual or couple overcome this negativity. It is also for you to decide whether or not you want to do the work. This involves retraining your mind – and this book will show you how – so you are able to respond, rather than react to your natural instincts around divorce, be it fight (hire a kickass lawyer), flight (run away and avoid) or freeze (become paralysed with fear and do nothing). These mechanisms help you react to perceived threats, and are designed to protect you. But they instantly cause hormonal and bodily changes, such as a rise in cortisol (your body's main stress hormone), and too much can wreak havoc on your body – think weight gain, muscle weakness, severe fatigue, irritability, difficulty concentrating, high blood pressure and headaches... not what you need on top of a divorce, right?

Kindness is the antidote and it comes in the form of dopamine, the happy hormone – sounds weird in a divorce, but bear with me! You can encourage more of the happy hormone with small daily habits to support you and help you perceive the divorce life threats better, manage your cortisol levels and put a capital D on Dopamine. So where does divorce stress come from? I want to introduce to you the main perpetrators of divorce stress...

The Divorce Mind Monkeys (DMMs)

The DMMs are the loud, difficult, challenging, catastrophising, unhelpful and relentless thoughts that send us into divorce petrification. This lot featured so heavily in the early part of my divorce that one day I hit an anxiety wall hard, and stayed there for some time.

The DMMs are responsible for:

- Keeping you from sleeping

- Waking you up at any given hour
- Filling your body with cortisol (stress hormone)
- Saying and doing things you regret
- Divorce brain fog
- Life overwhelm
- Not trying things differently
- Crippling comparison
- Your thoughts of failure, shame and unworthiness
- Partaking of unhelpful food, alcohol and substances
- Addictive tendencies
- Loneliness and feelings of being unloved
- Growing anger, resentment and bitterness
- Parental comparison and failings
- Future thoughts of being alone and penniless
- Keeping you in automatic pilot mode

Automatic pilot mode is the state in which we live and operate for most of our lives. It is how we function when travelling from A to B and we forget how we got there. It is not being conscious of what we are saying, doing or thinking, leading us to react rather than respond. Automatic pilot is a mode of living where we are 'doing' rather than 'being'. Divorce conflict can be ramped up when we're operating in this way, and it is fertile ground for conflict, misunderstandings and overthinking rather than feeling into what is happening. Becoming more aware of how you live is key to living more peacefully, 'kindfully' and with more joy (even in divorce). Meditation is a practice that can be incredibly helpful to assist in your transition from automatic pilot to being more aware. If you want to begin reducing the DMMs' participation through your divorce decisions and actions, please download my free Taster Mindfulness and Meditation Course (see the Divorce Goddess link in the Resources section).

We'll delve more deeply into the DMMs and how to deal with them throughout the book. Things that the DMMs are not responsible for (permit me a drum roll) are...

YOUR CHOICES!

The sooner you choose to rein the DMMs back in and feel more in control – which also allows you to be more present, focused and purposeful – the less they have space to create negativity.

And believe me... the DMMs love to create conflict.

Which is why you'll be asked many times in this book to check in with them, notice what effect they're having on your thoughts, words and actions, and take back control by creating new habits and maybe changing other parts of your life in the process.

About This Book

This book is firstly and most importantly an inspirational guidebook of hope and possibilities. I share insights from my 15+ years of therapist and coaching experience, plus inspiration from my clients (whose names have been changed) with supportive, progressive and less conflictual ways for you to 'flip' the way you view your divorce and how you may choose to behave through it. It is my ultimate and heartfelt wish that you'll have a kinder, more compassionate and accepting divorce so your future is not defined by negative, damaging conflict, but by a harmonious, kinder experience on which you can build the next chapter of your life.

It is also a practical book. I'll guide you through six stages, laid out in three parts – Kinder Foundations, A Kinder Journey and A Kinder Outcome – so that, no matter where you are in the process, you'll be supported to be able to negotiate and renegotiate with kindness rather than conflict, and set yourself on a gentler, more forgiving path of understanding and kindness. This process is for women, men, same-sex couples and childless couples... in fact, it is for anyone of any age who is confronting the truth, the reality and the scary prospect of a breakup, separation or divorce.

Kinder Foundations – the basis of anything that we want to build well

We build houses, plan life-changing events like moving home and create work projects – all with a plan in mind, with a group of experts or support squad, and our vision. So why should divorce be any different, other than the conditioning around it that has anchored the whole process in fear, shame and failure? Why do couples go blindly into the headlights without a project plan, clear ideas or a sustainable process applied with kindness to reduce conflict that's going to work for them? Because it's not the norm. With courts rammed to capacity with divorcing couples, is it not time to turn the tide, literally change the course of separation and divorce by cultivating something that is kind, compassionate and less conflictual?

When we work with kindness and compassion in divorce, we have more opportunities to mitigate relationship disaster and anxiety; stress is reduced, and there's less likelihood of financial ruin. In this Part of the book we will gather together what you know, identify what you don't know, and begin to create a framework on which to get you through your separation or divorce with some semblance of grace, dignity, healing and empowerment.

A Kinder Journey – well, if you're going to do it, do it well!

Ask yourself right now: do you want to be that person in years' time who is still angry, still sitting in Victim Land (because you know you'll hate it), and still waiting and wanting to eradicate the divorce years rather than seeing them as a time of learning, self-discovery and healing? As with any journey, you may be rewarded with solid-gold moments that light up your day like a beautiful sunrise or leave you feeling blessed with an early night! There will be times where you'll want to rest, hide in bed and mend, and give yourself permission to feel lost, sad or vulnerable. You may not want to carry on. But there will also be times where you dust yourself down, put your best face towards the sun and get back on the path.

This Part contains valuable tools and guidance to help you navigate the rollercoaster of emotions, unexpected trials and magical winning moments. Treat it like a map – when you use it, you risk less of the negative feelings and getting even more lost.

A Kinder Outcome – it's all about you!

The final Part explores the rewards that come from the work, be it emotional, mental, spiritual or physical – they are for you to enjoy, savour and be proud of. We think that nothing good ever happens to us when we're in the thick of hard and painful stuff, but it does. We just need to get out of our own way, trust more in the bigger picture and let go of how we think things are going to pan out. Trust that good stuff happens to good people.

Keeping up with the practices, using the tools and creating your parachute to use when you need it is what this Part is all about: taking control of the DMMs streaming fear into your life, and owning every part of who you are and celebrating it, over and over again. You do get to thrive rather than survive when you do the work on yourself. It comes back and touches other parts of your life you never realised at the time that it could – like happy, well-balanced children, solid future relationships, and the gift that is a more peaceful mind, body, heart and soul.

Embarking on Your Divorce Journey

Journeys are evolutionary for all of us – they are how we learn. Try to see your divorce journey as your evolution and an opportunity to change the way you think, act and speak in your scary new world. If your divorce feels like you've been dropped into a jungle, into a desert or onto a polar ice cap (choose your location) with a meagre ration pack, several children, your Ex, your pets, and your family and friends, with no map to get home, you're not alone. Your divorce experience is about you owning your part in the process of getting everyone to the final destination in one piece, together, with your health, sense of humour and any sense of hope for a more compassionate future left intact. Be open to change and possibilities and, as with anything new, use the lessons learned to set the best foundations for your new life.

While this book is about finding the places where kindness for conflict can make a difference, it is also a reminder that your needs matter, and through the practice of self-kindness you will begin to clearly and confidently know what they are and how to ask for them. It is my greatest wish that this book becomes a useful map for you, a companion for those 3-in-the-morning, gut-aching wake-ups; for an inspiring read on the train ride to work; or while waiting for your children's after-school clubs to end. It is here for you to work with and explore. Your divorce is a journey of self-discovery; it can be as challenging as you choose to make it ("What about my Ex?!!" – I hear you, but bear with me!). Simply, your divorce is about YOU, who you are and how you walk, trip, stumble, crawl or sprint along your own path. Only you have ownership of your thoughts, words and actions, and no one can take that away from you – not even your Ex.

Choosing a Kinder Divorce

Divorce gives us a choice each and every day: you can take a left turn or right one, good or bad, positive or negative, each choice giving you the opportunity to do something differently. You can negotiate with kindness, courage and not be afraid of conflict.

Kindness For Conflict

I saw a newly ploughed field as a metaphor for my divorced life. A large field filled with big furrows of dark-brown clay mud; the kind of sticky mud that clings to your boots and continues to get heavier as you walk. Sometimes you can kick off some of the mud, and for a while you feel a little lighter. So this divorce field was one where I instinctively felt I needed to walk slowly rather than run; in fact, I realised I had very little choice with this decision, as my life journey now included a lot of time here. Life had pushed me off the smoother path and I had to learn to walk differently, being a whole lot more present.

I knew that if I cheated and walked down a furrow, trying to find a sneaky way through, that at some point I would still have to cross the rest of the furrows. There are no shortcuts through this field of divorce. I did try the 'life cheat' option several times, thinking I would find an easier walk around the edge of the field… and yep, I got sent back to cross those old furrows to experience and learn from them again.

The newly ploughed field is fertile ground for learning, growth and an awareness of your life and who you are. Gently embrace the day-to-day sticky challenges, which, when they drop off your boots, allow the lighter moments in life, those gifts of hopeful moments, to present themselves.

If you're rushing at your usual 100 miles an hour, impatient and 'wanting it now' life, divorce has this funny way of slowing you down. This field is here to teach you about life – you have a choice to be aware of your good decisions, appreciate the easier days and focus on how to improve on or learn from the heavier, longer and sadder ones.

No matter what path you decide to take in the form of separation or divorce, it is invariably met with painful, heart-wrenching emotions, which everyone is unprepared for.

As a client, Simon, said: "I was used to feeling in control, making decisions in the workplace and everything getting done when I wanted. Divorce taught me early on that I was going to have to get used to feeling pretty much out of control most of the time and, ironically, the more I embraced 'letting go' and being less controlling, the easier it became."

So… are you ready to begin? 'Kindness for Conflict' is about accepting and letting go rather than feeling resigned and holding on. Hold this thought throughout the book. Let's go!

Part 1

Kinder Foundations

Hope, acceptance and forgiveness are the firm ground for kindness winning over conflict. I believe that coming back to the tenets of being a compassionate, big-hearted human being is what you always have a choice over. It begins with you, every time.

In this Part, I'll take you through the reasons why building kinder foundations will ultimately serve you going forwards, by reducing conflict and saving you from years of carrying post-divorce anger, victimhood, trust issues and dating disappointments. I'll show you why creating positive neural pathways and healing old negative habits can prevent you from being triggered further by narcissistic or controlling behaviours by your Ex. These may include unpredictable changes in schedules, left-field emails and messages designed to cause harm. Unpredictability, lack of commitment from your Ex, painful words and the unkindest blows below the belt concerning your children can be the biggest causes of anxiety. Your divorce-knackered mind can so easily become your own torture chamber the longer time you spend ruminating, so is it time for you to decide this will no longer be the case? Is your challenge to begin to believe that when you apply kinder foundations, you can get through this with your mind, body, heart and soul intact?

Building kinder foundations is all about creating a safe, strong and positive place for you to operate from to reduce divorce fallout, get your head clear and be prepared for whatever is coming. You will be more unshakeable, and have the tools to remain calm and resilient. Remember: you can't control your Ex, but you have ultimate control over what you say, how your divorce mind monkeys (DMMs) are behaving, and your actions.

In this Part we begin to lay out a framework for you to start building upon – one that challenges societal thinking around divorce and creates a space that is conducive to kindness rather than conflict.

So – are you ready?

Time to take that deep breath in and then out… you've got this! Say it loud and proud: "I am powerful and, yes, I can do the hard stuff."

Chapter 1

Self-Kindness

Self-kindness – such as having an early night, drinking more water, focusing on yourself for a while or taking a holiday – is often something we feel we don't have the time, money, inclination or permission for. It's something we seem to fall short of – especially during separation or divorce, when it is most needed. Negative thoughts like failure, shame and guilt, thrown at us by the divorce mind monkeys (DMMs), seem to stick, so why would we nurture, nourish or attend to ourselves when we are feeling less than worthy of such care?

For many of you going through separation and divorce, there may be no thought of self-kindness at all… and then you wonder why you've hit the hard, unwavering and unforgiving wall of exhaustion, depression and anxiety; the conflict-driven, sleep-deprived, shouty, hangry, divorce-brain-fogged general f*ckedness.

I was the chief commander of No Self-Kindness until I hit the wall, and hit it hard. I was in the middle of making a cup of tea one day, when for no apparent reason I couldn't keep the tears locked inside any longer and they flowed for, um, about six hours. I thought I had lost it: I hadn't, I just needed to attend to myself, to care and pay attention to my needs a little more.

Self-kindness doesn't need to be difficult. Self-kindness is simply putting your mental, emotional, spiritual (yes, a little 'woo woo' is here too) and physical oxygen mask on first, every day. It is about committing and sticking to even one powerful habit – think stopping calling yourself an idiot and praising yourself instead, drinking hot water with lemon in the morning, getting into bed early, or making time to gift yourself a lovely long bath instead of a quick shower.

If you're unclear why self-kindness is so important when going through a divorce, consider the following, which can occur due to a lack of self-kindness. Are any of these familiar?

- **Mental fog:** Unable to focus, stressed, anxious, unable to sleep, overwhelmed, head achingly full of thoughts, no peace
- **Emotional mess:** Depressed, angry, resentful, ashamed, guilty, grief-stricken, sad, heartbroken

- **Lack of purpose:** Stuck in a rut, spiritually adrift, lacking in intuition, not grounded, not feeling yourself
- **Physical regret:** Sluggish (I love and hate that word), hungover, dehydrated, hungry/hangry, tired, unwell, overweight, underweight, abusing cigarettes, alcohol or drugs, aching limbs, headachy

Ultimately it is up to you how you want to feel, and I recommend applying lots of self-kindness and self-love. It may take days, weeks or months before you sign up to be kind to yourself, but try to say goodbye to self-flagellation and self-punishment because that DOES NOT work in the long term. Instead, you're going to learn to care for yourself, have your own back and be your own keeper.

Kimberley found my work on Instagram and said it was the 'kindness' element she wanted in her divorce, but she thought her Ex might make this outcome difficult to achieve. We chatted about how her divorce was not about her Ex, it was about her and she had a choice – to empower herself and use kindness, or not.

As you will discover in this chapter, self-kindness can reach the deepest level of your humanity, the place where the dark, hurtful bits you avoid and dismiss, reside. Self-kindness, along with hope, acceptance and forgiveness, are the foundations for a kinder divorce. Understanding the importance of this, sitting with and contemplating this as early on as you can, will provide you with a firmer ground to take you through the separation process with more kindness and less conflict. Honestly though, if you are already in the darkest night of the soul, why not take a look at your most challenging moments afresh, recognise how strong you are already and begin taking smaller, kinder steps into the places you may fear to tread.

In this chapter, I gently encourage you to look at:

- What ended your marriage
- Why divorce is an opportunity to learn to sail in these stormy seas rather than stay angry and scared in your harbour
- How to feel your feelings and let them all out rather than hold them in
- What your go-to coping strategy and defence mechanism is (you may be surprised – I was!)
- How to have the hardest conversation in the world with those you love
- Why having a trusted team of professionals/support squad around you is a necessity rather than optional

And to remember – you are enough.

An Ending: Dealing with Grief

It all begins with an ending...

The ending of your marriage can come about from either party meeting that 'someone' or maybe one day you wake up and realise your marriage is no longer where you want to be. You may be the couple who look at each other and decide that the route of anger and unresolvable differences, loneliness and irritation is no longer for you. You might not like the ending and the ending might not like you, but you are where you are, and the path of an unknown future and huge personal change is waiting for you to step onto it.

How the divorce conversation happens impacts on your initial thoughts about how you want to move forward through the process. Whether it happens via a text, a heated argument or a planned conversation, the emotional floodgates will open up – and with your emotions come the DMMs. Those pesky, difficult, challenging and conflictual thoughts that mess with your head when you least expect it – that trigger you to act or speak in a way based on them rather than the reality.

What do you do with the tsunami of thoughts going round in your head, and the one-billion-dollar question: how do you move forward?

Endings ask us to look at what worked, what didn't and why, and how we can learn moving forwards. We do this by looking at the tough stuff: the DMM thoughts and feelings that unexpectedly appear; the life-changing decisions we're asked to make under such stress on every level.

Grief is about dealing with *loss*. Think if you can for a moment about the loss of your marriage and life as you knew it. Could you not only mourn it, but also celebrate the good parts – children, successful ventures, the learning from it, the commitment of time spent together? You may feel like you just want to bury it all for good, but try to remember the parts that worked, that were cohesive and why they worked. In everything there is light and dark. We are able to truly see the good and the light when we're faced with the bad and are in darkness. Without dark, we wouldn't know light. Consider this lovely quote from Martin Luther King: "Darkness cannot drive out darkness: only light can do that. Hate cannot drive out hate: only love can do that."

Through her work in the support of grief and personal trauma, Dr Elisabeth Kübler-Ross (for more information, see the Resources section) gave us the five stages of grief model:

- Denial
- Anger
- Bargaining
- Depression

- Acceptance

A wise friend shared this five-stage model with me. She told me to read it and see where I was at so I could begin the process of understanding why I was feeling the way I was feeling, acting the way I was acting, and making sense of that thought tsunami in my head. I was then struck by a rare divorce lightbulb moment: If I was feeling like this, then wouldn't my soon-to-be Ex? I said this to my friend, and she asked me to think about it; I jokingly said, "I don't really care." She gave me 'that' look and said nothing. Later, reflecting on our conversation, I realised we all need to care about how other people feel, especially when they are the other parent of your children and someone who you are going to be travelling this future journey with.

Here are my interpretations of Kübler-Ross's five stages of grief, in relation to divorce:

- **Denial:** It's not happening, I'm in a living nightmare and I'll soon wake up; this is just how we are and we'll bounce back. Welcome to the shame, shock and fear rabbit hole.
- **Anger:** It's Fight Club central, with a lot of hate and frustration – I'm gathering an army, dishing out punishments for marital crimes and broken principles, and shouting a big f*ck you.

- **Bargaining:** I'm balancing 'let's try to be nice' versus 'let's not try to be nice' while wondering what to do now; where do I stand, where is this going to lead, where is the meaning in it all and what do I do next?

- **Depression:** This is my life now, I feel like a failure; I feel a sense of hopelessness, loneliness and despair; it feels like a Groundhog Day; I am overwhelmed, exhausted and it is relentless.

- **Acceptance:** OMG, I just had a light bulb moment and feel a tiny bit better. I'm giving myself permission to actually feel that I may have just turned a small corner; I can see a potential new life and I am open to options. I have an idea of a plan to put in place, the days seem a little brighter and I think I'm moving on.

Unless you both wanted a divorce at the same time, your Ex may be at a different stage of grief to you. They may also move through the stages more slowly if they're more resistant to the divorce, or at an anger-inducingly fast pace if they've had more time to process the decision to divorce. Being at different stages of grief can throw you both out of sync (as if there wasn't enough to manage), and this is where the DMMs can go from having a party to staging a year-long festival in your head. (This is what I think of as 'divorce hangover material' – if we don't look after ourselves with kindness, the divorce process is going to hurt a whole lot more and it's going to be tougher for the children.)

Try this: If your Ex is not up for sharing this Kindness for Conflict process with you, you might want to think about where they are anyway to understand where they are on their journey. This can be helpful in terms of how you choose to communicate moving forwards, irrespective of your Ex's thoughts on this. Just because they don't want to participate, that doesn't mean to say that you can't!

Begin to listen to yourself, those spidery thoughts, those butterfly whispers, your gut instinct. This is your superpower.

The key to a kinder, less conflictual divorce lies in choice. Not one person in your world can take this away from you unless you give them permission to. You can choose to tear down what you shared with anger and bitterness while hurting what's left of the life you had together (such as your children), or you can choose to rebuild your new future pragmatically, constructively and compassionately. If your intention is for a kinder divorce, understanding and applying self-kindness is the way forward: it is the underpinning of something far more powerful than falling further into conflict.

The Beginning: Setting Your Intention

Here is an idea for you to think about from the inspirational author and self-development speaker Dr Wayne Dyer. Can your intention create your reality? In other words, can you achieve what you want, such as a kinder divorce experience, if you make it your intention and do 'the work' to achieve it, even if it's just for you? When I came across this concept, I loved the opportunity to really get out of my divorce box and do things differently by taking control of my thoughts!

Setting your own positive intention is an opportunity for you to create a powerful contract with yourself and make a personal commitment to have a kinder rather than a conflictual divorce. I am inviting you to think and then write about how you would like to feel, how you want to live each day and how you want to show up in your divorce.

You will be called to dig deep into your strength, stubbornness and determination. There will be times when the fears of family, friends and children will wobble you. Expectations of a fight/battle are normal, which is why setting an intention about the experience that you want to have is important. Your DMMs will try and validate you having a combative divorce on the bad days – this is human nature. However, your positive intention is a powerful tool to keep you in balance and facing your true North on difficult days: it holds the DMMs to account so you can proceed with what you believe and feel to be right and good for you and your family, which is ultimately a kinder approach.

Your Divorce Intention provides you with an opportunity to take control of and own your choices, no matter what is said, how others behave and what they think (this includes your Ex, your friends and your family). If you decide that you're not going to have a divorce battle and that instead you will commit to minimal family distress and destruction (rather than fuel society's automatic expectations of divorce discontent), then why not make this more likely to happen by setting your Intention?

I want to share my own Divorce Intention, which I wrote one night, thinking about the possibilities of a kinder divorce:

"I, Tosh Brittan, on this day, 24th September, write a commitment to myself, my family, my Ex and our community to be the kindest, best and biggest-hearted person I can be through my divorce. I will see my divorce as an opportunity and a positive life project, by trying to be mindful of my thoughts, words and actions. I will try to mend the bits and old thought processes that no longer serve me as I go through the divorce – like anger, fear and disappointment – and I commit to growing my self-confidence and self-worth, so I feel more empowered.

I will invest in myself with good support, commit to learning new ways of 'doing life' and I will show up every day for me. I will try to be kind to myself so I am able to be kind, loving and compassionate towards my Ex and this process we are all about to go through. I commit to trusting that my Ex and I will both come through this period of time in our lives with our beloved children, dignity and health intact. In the future, I want to be able to celebrate, feel a sense of achievement and be proud of how I divorced.

And finally, I want our children to see that kindness, love and friendship can come out of sad, difficult and challenging life events."

I reread this to myself a lot while going through my divorce. A couple of times I screwed it up in frustration and anger – this stuff can be hard! But a small voice inside kept telling me to stick with it, to trust in the process of being kind and to believe in the goodness that is inherent in all of us, that can come through when we hold space for it. Reading my Divorce Intention still brings tears to my eyes.

Try this: Writing your Divorce Intention.

- Find somewhere quiet, somewhere you feel safe, and get cosy and comfortable.

- Take several deep breaths, focusing on your breath as you breathe in and out through your nose, breathing down into your belly, triggering your body's natural relaxation response.

- Think about how you want to feel in one year, five years or ten years' time. How would you like your life to look after your divorce?

- Begin to freely write your Intention without any pressure for it to be perfect – you can adjust it in the days ahead. Allow the words to flow, try not to overthink. Write from your heart (not your head) and give yourself permission to think of the best scenarios and the kindest possibilities. Honestly ask yourself how much you're willing to invest in yourself to keep your Intention for a kinder divorce strong, so that your actions going forward both mirror and support your Intention and ultimately those you love most.

You may like to use the following phrases to help you get started:

- I commit to experiencing my divorce… (openly, honestly, kindly)

- During my divorce, I am feeling… (empowered, confident, authentic, strong)

- I release… (certain thoughts, emotions, patterns of behaviour)

- I give myself the gift of... (peace, kinder conversations, self-care)
- I promise myself I will always try to... (fully listen, respond rather than react, speak kindly to myself)

When writing your Intention, just let the words (and tears) flow – don't force them, just let them come. It may feel slightly surreal writing about the good stuff you want in your divorce, but out of the ashes comes the phoenix and out of the mud grows a lotus! It is up to you whether you wish to stay where you are or to have the courage to believe your Intention is possible.

Make it a regular or even daily habit to read your Divorce Intention to yourself and immerse yourself in the possibilities of the words you have chosen. You *can* do this divorce business differently. Making self-kindness a daily habit as you walk this path is the nourishment you have available to support yourself.

Committing to yourself is where you begin the process of self-empowerment in your divorce. Your Intention helps you focus to work on your triggers – like impatience, anger or wanting to control things.

You may want to send your Divorce Intention to your Ex, or ask them if they want to read it with a view to writing one too. They may choose not to – they may be unsure and untrusting, and that's okay – but remember, your divorce is about *your* experience, not your Ex's. If your Ex decides not to write (or share) their Intention, they may still 'get it'; it may land somewhere. Even though you are two people with different personalities and come to the divorce process with differences of opinion, you can both work towards the possibility of a kinder divorce from different perspectives.

Work towards your positive Intention every day and trust that the small actions of kindness have a ripple effect. Just try not to let the DMMs tell you otherwise. This is new ground for them and they will be resistant to change because they want to protect you – but they aren't always right!

For more in depth guidance, live coaching and support on this, you might want to take a look at the six-week Kindness for Conflict Divorce Support Course (details at the Divorce Goddess link in the Resources section).

Feeling the Feelings

Each and every one of us is uniquely different. We all have our own individual ways of understanding the reasons behind why divorce or separation happens. Divorce is a whole heap of emotions, processes and life situations that many of us lack any preparation for, in any way, shape or form. It hits you like a steam train and blows apart your life as you know it.

One mum in the school carpark declared, "Divorce is the most f*cking horrendous thing you will ever go through." In that statement was a wonderful degree of clarity, which I found surprisingly helpful. It comforted my overactive, worried imagination, giving me permission to feel the way I felt and be with my experience rather than denying it.

So, why is it important to embrace the painful, difficult and challenging parts and accept that it's normal to have them?

Looking carefully at your feelings gives you permission to properly feel them, and to notice when the DMMs want you to lock them away. When the fear, anger and resentment monkeys have your feelings locked away, they have the power to release them when you're least expecting to feel that fear, anger or resentment – at the school gate, in the workplace, at home or with your Ex. The DMMs can also save them for special occasions – celebrations and new experiences – in other words, they can use your unexplored fears to bring you crashing down, and fast.

Sweeping feelings under the carpet is understandable – it's a natural response our minds use to protect ourselves. We go into denial and minimise what's happening (something I explore more in the next section, 'How to Cope'), and it becomes easier to fill this space with unhelpful habits like eating unhealthy food or spending hours on social media when we feel lonely, angry or sad. The trouble is, at some point you need to look at that stuff under the carpet, otherwise those fears and worries will grow: think mountains and molehills when the DMMs get involved!

If you're thinking you want to skip past this process of really feeling your feelings, PLEASE DON'T! It's hard to look at challenging feelings when you feel so raw, but it's necessary – and helpful. By feeling your feelings, you're allowing them to help you have the experience that's needed to be able to heal. Feeling your feelings lets the good stuff in (because you worked through the tough stuff and made some room) and it moves you forward towards the beautiful green luscious valley that is your future (or whatever your goal location looks like!).

Throughout the stages of separation and divorce, I recommend you regularly give yourself some time to feel your feelings.

Try this: Here are some of the ways that have worked for me and my clients to get you started on feeling the feelings:

- **Get loud and sweary.** Take yourself off somewhere where you can't be heard – outside or in the car is always good (without the children, of course!) – and shout very loudly, scream like a banshee, holler and swear to your heart's content. Give yourself permission to get some of what you need to say out of your system, as loudly as you need to!

- **Write them out.** Write them, jot, doodle and scribble down everything you're feeling – every word, thought or emotion that comes into your head. You may want to use different colours to write certain words about the current week's frustration, sadness, blame, guilt and shame. You can also look back through your journal and see how far you have come on those harder days. Or you might prefer to write a frank letter to your Ex – just don't send it. Writing is cathartic (and in fact is how my blog started) because it gives you the chance to brain-dump the things that are emotionally overloading you.

- **Cry.** Get into your bed, go and be somewhere safe, with a supersize tissue box to hand, and cry. You may have done this many times already, but I would prescribe it again and again to let out your anger, sadness and feelings of failure. Cry however you need to – silent big tears, body-wrenching fear-filled sobbing, desperate gut-twisting crying... just cry and think again – your letting go is making space for better things coming.

- **Get physical.** Start running, go to the gym or have a long walk. Create a 'just for you to cry and be utterly miserable to' playlist or throw some moves around your kitchen; many a divorcee has done some serious letting go this way! Dance like nobody's watching and shake it out, cry and laugh while you're doing it, and see how you feel afterwards.

Divorce is like an onion – each time you really feel your feelings, see it as an opportunity to shed a layer. This is your own healing work and an opportunity for self-kindness. It encourages you to get to know yourself better and to become more aware of how you feel afterwards: alive and light, or exhausted and perhaps in need of more self-care. You may also find this process easier or more difficult depending on whether you've slept and eaten well, drunk enough water, felt lonely or unwell, or had an argument with your Ex. Whatever you feel now is right for you right now: accept and feel your feelings and allow yourself to have them. They make you real, human and the loving person you are.

My client Helen shared that her experience of 'feeling her feelings' was her lightbulb moment. She said that each day when she went to work, she locked her emotions in a box and put the box on a shelf in her office. She said it was the easiest way to deal with them. However, it was harder after a Monday morning school playground chat with the other mums. All she heard was the 'happy families' chat about the weekend. I asked why she put herself through this when it made her feel this way? Could she empower herself by choosing to spend this time differently and instead go for a walk or journal why she felt the way she did? She did this for a couple of months until she felt stronger; the chats still stung, but she wasn't so upset by them. Helen said, "I learned that life was tougher if I didn't feel and be with my feelings. If I popped them into a box trying to forget them, they would still exist, mainly inside me; they would grow, fester and stay with me."

How to Cope

Divorce is an opportunity to get to know yourself, reconnect to your 'inner strength' that you learned way before all this divorce stuff happened, and get better at responding rather than reacting. Get in there! I'm talking defence mechanisms and coping strategies – the stuff that's good to have some clue about, especially when your Ex is on the other end of the thought process kicking your Achilles heel. Understanding and being super-aware of how you think, speak and (re)act is like having a superpower. To be able to calm stormy waters as opposed to drowning in them is the hallelujah gateway to a calmer, wiser and more conscious you!

Think of the times when you have reacted rather than responded – think losing it with your Ex rather than being cool and choosing your battles. Each time you make a wiser, calmer choice of words or actions, it's like removing a layer of stress all by yourself. It's empowering to have this inside knowledge of ourselves; it's the part we can dip into when we're unsure which way to turn (common in divorce!). Getting 100% behind fully knowing YOU is the kinder path to empowerment through your divorce. Let's face it; we need all the help we can get in the divorce business and, as with everything, it begins with you!

Knowing when to accept and let go of what you can't control, such as snarky comments from your Ex, rather than being resigned and holding on to them is a big part of changing the way you 'do' a kinder divorce.

So how do you get good at noticing when you aren't coping? Or stopping yourself from falling into the usual arguments? Do you hate yourself for not accepting, letting go and committing to a gentler life of less verbal self-flagellation? Do you carry on doing what you're doing? Freud defined insanity as doing the same thing over and over again and expecting a different result. This can lead to more anxiety, depression and staying stuck where you are. If you're done with feeling like this, I encourage you to begin a daily habit of checking in with yourself (set an alarm if you need reminding). Practise taking deep breaths when you feel an overwhelming sense of emotion coming up, or take time out to sit quietly somewhere comfortable with no distractions for just five minutes. Get into the habit of noticing when you're on automatic pilot (the absent-minded thought-based mode mentioned in the Introduction) and become the observer of your thoughts, rather than being in amongst them (divorce fog). This is how you begin to build a protective buffer of mindful awareness so you begin responding rather than reacting (you are in rather than out of control – more on this in the section 'Your Relationship with Your Ex' in Chapter 2). It is easier to become triggered when you're doing the daily automatic pilot grind and get caught off guard or surprised, which is when you lose it and hate yourself. Becoming more self-aware means you're more likely to stay in your power and feel a sense of accomplishment that you held your sh*t together! Feels a better option, right?

Understanding how you respond to difficult situations can also be really helpful in other areas of your life and helps you understand others better too.

Identifying your current coping strategy

What is your go-to defence mechanism or coping strategy? If you can identify with one (or several) from the following examples you now have an opportunity to use this knowledge and take kinder steps in conflict. You can become responsive, knowing how you 'work', rather than react. This is where you want to be heading.

Try this: Before doing any work on yourself, I suggest you make time so you aren't disturbed, get yourself a lovely cup of tea or a warm drink, and take a few deep breaths. You might want to use this as an opportunity to practise being present by trying a new flavour tea and checking in with your senses by feeling the warmth, smelling the aroma, noticing when your mind wanders off (that's what they do) and bringing your attention back to the experience of you and your cup of tea. Practising being present with what you are doing is training your DMMs to do what you want them to do.

Take a moment to jot down any observations you have as you read on. Are you ready?

First up is DENIAL! This is easy to fall into, especially if you're in shock. Denial is not accepting the reality of your relationship being over, so you may find yourself thinking, "My Ex is having a midlife crisis" or "It's just a phase", resulting in you not making practical changes as you stick your head in the sand. So how could this affect your divorce? By giving more time to the DMMs trying to protect you from divorce danger, you may inadvertently end up feeling more fear, anger and shame – it is fertile ground for growing frustration and anger towards your Ex – resulting in more lawyer's letters and decisions based on rage rather than an amicable partnership – and can end up costing you both financially and emotionally.

Ah, the MINIMISER – my old friend! This one is where the pain is being denied – call it eternal optimism – with thoughts like, "If I keep super-positive, everything is going to be okay" and "It's going to be fine, it will all work out". Putting a brave face on the situation can lead to you bottling up pain and emotions and packing them away for later, perhaps surfacing as illness and mental breakdown, or coming out in your next relationship, rather than acknowledging them and letting them out. I recommend therapy, coaching or counselling during your breakup, but if it's not for you at this time then at least begin writing your thoughts in a journal; get them out of your head onto the paper and remember, it's okay to not be okay. (My tearstained notebooks are a testament to this!)

Will realised his go-to defence mechanism and coping strategy was to minimise everything. He lived in a good area, he had been married for 16 years, he had three great kids in good schools, a holiday home in Majorca and a successful career, and he thought life was wonderful. He couldn't face what was happening after he found out his wife was having an affair with a dad at the school. When the horrifying, shaming news came out, he would publicly say, "It's not that bad, I'll be fine." Except he wasn't; he was far from fine – he confided he was "terrified and exhausted, trying to keep it all together" and that he felt like "a swan on speed", with no one offering to help him because he seemed okay on the surface (whereas underneath...). Coaching empowered Will to get better at asking for help. We created a self-care plan and he started writing his thoughts down (he now swears by journaling) so he had 'headspace' to manage his emotions better, accept what happened and be less hard on himself.

ANGER is a natural emotion and is designed to protect us. Try to see your anger as a strengthening emotion you can use to fuel the positive parts of your divorce such as good co-parenting and productive meetings, rather than the negative parts like retaliation, retribution and more conflict. Use the anger you feel to do something constructive rather than destructive – redirect it to training for a marathon or retraining for your ideal job – use it to support you, not bring you down. Notice when you're most feeling angry and put a pair of trainers on to work it out rather than get even. Misplaced anger can so often result in you feeling guilty, alienated and having a tougher, more conflictual divorce as a result.

DISPLACEMENT is all about putting the divorce oxygen mask on everyone else first, resulting in you suffering more. If you find yourself saying, "I'm okay but I'm worried about the children" or you're 'mother henning' everyone else, you're going to feel the divorce emotions more. One day you may wake up and realise you are not okay; you're exhausted, with no real foundations of self-kindness, and you may find yourself hitting a wall. This can result in you becoming ill, feeling depressed and running on empty. Instead, you need to help and support yourself. Do something lovely for yourself each day... start small... perhaps with a morning cup of tea, sitting quietly on your own, without devices, learning to be present with how you're feeling.

DIE-HARD/REACTIONARY – what you say and how you act is all about not facing up to what has happened. You may react by thinking, "Divorce is the best thing that could have happened – I've been wanting this for years!" Well, this may be true, but like anything we have to look at not only the good bits, but also the bad parts (no escaping, I'm afraid). If you just focus on what you thought you wanted for all those years, you're never going to look at the good parts and why you stayed (and the bad parts being the lessons?). You just focus on the outcome of where you are now, rather than honestly exploring what was right and what wasn't, and softening any hard edges around what happened to help you heal difficult emotions going forwards.

Here you may want to explore further, rediscover and understand why you think, behave and speak as you do. Perhaps use this as an opportunity to see where you have felt blocked in other areas of your life, or what's not working quite as well as it could do, and consider what you can do to change how you respond.

You can choose to have a life over fear.

Try this: Consider your coping mechanisms and how they impact your life.

I invite you to think about how you're coping at the moment, what the cost of coping like this is to you and others, and what the benefits are to you and others. For example, you may minimise your pain and say "I'm all good!" when asked about being a single parent, yet this can be far from the truth if you're not facing your fears of surviving as a single parent. Or maybe you never ask for help so your friends think you're okay and leave you to get on with it, saying "You're so strong!" while you gulp and think, "If you only knew!"

Write down your coping mechanism and then list how this impacts you and then impacts those you love. For example, you may get more stressed because no one really knows how you feel, so you get angry quickly. Next, list the benefits of the coping mechanism to yourself and others – just how well is this working for you? For example, some coping mechanisms may seem good at first because you don't have to face your fears or see your friends worrying about you.

You can repeat this exercise for any of the coping mechanisms to help you see a little more clearly exactly how they are working for you. As you continue to check in with yourself, you're building your self-awareness muscle rather than expecting all the challenges, difficulties and pain to miraculously disappear or get better on their own. It's the small daily habits that build your foundation of kindness – firstly for yourself, and then extending it to others. (You're going to be building on this as you progress through the book.)

There's a good chance that you have been using these coping mechanisms in life for a really long time; they're deeply embedded neural pathways. But, as with everything, you have a personal choice to make the adjustments suggested in this book to give you simple and better ways of coping as you move through the process or not! They're designed to retrain the DMMs, resulting in the amazing you becoming more aware and living more of your divorce life without feelings of fear, shame and failure.

Telling Those You Love

For many families and friends, divorce can be a big, freakin' deep, emotional crevasse – one filled with surprises and shocks. But it can garner 'blood is thicker than water' support if managed well. So, how do you go about telling those you love you're getting divorced?

Remember that when people talk to you about your divorce, it's often through their own life lens of experiences that comes with their own judgements, thoughts and fears. Be prepared for every response – love, understanding, "I told you so" condescension, or concerned questions about your children.

Family and friends

Before you begin, have your Intention to hand (refer to the earlier section 'The Beginning: Setting Your Intention'). Remember, it is your reference point and a guide in difficult times. You may find it helpful to give a copy of your Intention to the people you love so there's no wriggle room for them to do anything but support you because they know your Intention is to move forwards with kindness. If you go into the conversation with clarity, kindness and a strong Intention, there are fewer places for people's judgements and their own emotions to hang out in. Explain your plan and your commitment to the process of a kinder divorce, which allows them to grasp the focus and energy behind your words (let's be honest, some are going to find this concept difficult, especially if all they've ever heard is bad stuff about divorce). Ask for their love and support so you can stay on this kinder, less conflictual journey. People love to be asked for help – it makes them feel useful and is a win for everyone.

If you have children, they need to know they have family members, friends or godparents looking out for them too, especially when their mum or dad is having a tough day. It takes the pressure off the children and you, just knowing this.

Your parents and in-laws may find it particularly difficult to navigate your divorce. This may include the shame of telling their church group, golf club or community about your divorce, the changing mantlepiece – removing wedding photos – and what happens to their relationship with a loved son-/daughter-in-law going forward, plus the relationship with any grandchildren.

Take a moment to ask yourself: How would it feel for your parents to know that there wasn't going to be a fight, that they could proudly say to their maybe judgemental friends, "Yes, they are getting divorced but they are going to do it better"? What a gift and a beacon of light for others to think about the possibilities of a kinder divorce, instead of all the unpleasantness that comes with sharing another sad, angry and battle-filled divorce story.

Telling the children

This has to be up there as one of the hardest conversations ever – the DMMs are going to send you into massive guilt-ridden mode. It may be that you are a child of divorced parents and remember when you were told, or you recall hearing in school about your friend's parents splitting up and their reaction. You may remember all the times you were hurt, disappointed and scared by the unknown, and this is going to be there at the surface as you share the news with your children. Come back to your Intention so you are able to better manage your emotions (which, as we know, children's radars pick up on) for a more constructive, calmer and compassionate conversation.

Preparing for this conversation weighs heavily for many, leading to gut-wrenching feelings of guilt. Although it won't make it easier, aim to be with these feelings and accept that you're going to feel like the sh*ttest parent ever for a while. As a loving, caring and supportive parent, this is normal; it can't be helped. See it as an important lesson for your children to manage difficulties with kindness. Maybe the need to have this conversation has prevented you and your Ex from moving forward with your lives, perhaps because you felt that staying together for the children was the right thing to do. Seeing them through their difficult school years may have seemed like a positive way to cope, but children learn to live with a 'normal' that is parents in a challenging, unloving relationship, which may then become the blueprint for them in later life and their own relationships.

One client told me, having spent the last five years 'protecting' her children from the inevitable, that finally telling the children was surprisingly okay. She described the conversation as like releasing a pressure valve in all their lives. The children just said "okay" and "can we go and play now?" And that was basically it, she said: the relief was palpable.

There's no ideal way to have this conversation; you don't have a blueprint, as you have probably never done this before. The most important thing is that you keep your children's wellbeing firmly in mind as you tell them.

Try this: Here are some possibilities to consider for having the conversation:

- Book a day as a family together with nothing else planned.
- Get yourselves outside if possible to feel more open and less 'trapped'. But include lots of cuddles and hugs!
- Don't include alcohol or stimulants like coffee/sugary drinks, which increase the stress hormone cortisol. Have 'the chat' after a meal so feeling 'hangry' isn't a factor.
- If you're stressed, try doing some exercise, meditation or have a walk beforehand.
- Have a pre-planned conversation with your Ex so you are both in a position to talk calmly and cohesively and stick to it.
- Hold on to your Intention for a kinder divorce; keep it in mind and remember that this conversation is for your children, not you.
- Explain that you still love each other; however, you're not *in love* with each other anymore.
- If they ask what's going to happen (older children may ask) regarding homes, pets, schools and friends, at least have an idea so you don't leave them hanging.
- Tell them that, no matter what happens, they are loved very much by you both and always will be.

- Tell them (many times if you have to) that they haven't done anything wrong and the separation has nothing to do with them.
- Don't argue with your Ex or have a dig – it's not cool on any level. This chat is about your children.
- DO NOT tell your children about affairs – let this be for another, much later conversation (if ever).
- DO NOT OVERTHINK THINGS!

If your Ex is not on the same page as you when it comes to telling your children, you may find that you are having this conversation on your own. It may or may not be easier to have this conversation on your own – everyone is different. If you are going it alone, consider these additional ideas to see if they might work for you:

- Write a plan of what to say to cover what may or may not change after the separation and when they are going to see the other parent (if possible). If you are able to have a discussion with your Ex before this conversation, let them know what you're telling the children so there are no future miscommunications. Both of you need to get on the same page for your children, if you can.
- Get cosy on the sofa, get bundled up with blankets, create a warm, safe and nurturing space.

- Have another family member or friend who the children love there to support you.

- Resist the desire to trash the other parent (I talk about this further in Chapter 5).

- Explain that you will both be there for them and that you both love them… a lot.

Remember: Children have radars – they can smell untruths before we have said them.

Children want to know that they are still going to be loved, fed and have somewhere safe to live.

As a child of divorced parents, I still remember the conversation they had with me, and I'm not convinced it ever leaves, so it's better for your kids to have an okay memory than a terrible one. Again, this really comes back to self-kindness, reducing guilt and therapy costs for your children and yourself. This is kindness to those you love, your Ex and yourself and is what you have control and a choice over: for you (both) to do it as well as you can.

Rallying Your Support Squad

Divorce can take every single scrap of rug out from under your feet in terms of feeling safe, held and part of something – no matter whether you left the relationship or were left. Nothing quite prepares you for the feelings of isolation, alienation and the creeping sense of loneliness that can sneak up when you least expect it before, during and after a relationship breakup. (I go more into the dreaded loneliness in the section 'Making Loneliness Your Friend' in Chapter 3.)

Here we look at who you need, want and can trust, and why getting your support squad together is going to get you into the confident and purposeful right space to make kinder choices moving forwards. We're talking friends and professionals – how to choose them, how to check in with your intuition, and why using 'pub lawyers' (mates who've been through this), and the 'been there, done that, got the T-shirt' social media therapists are not always helpful for a kinder and less conflictual divorce!

Friends

Our friends are our kindred spirits, the 'calling out the BS-moments' crew and the ones who help keep us sane. But I want to caveat friends with this: no one knows what it is truly like to get a divorce unless they have been through one themselves, and every divorce is different. Going through separation isn't something everyone gets or fully understands – no matter how brilliant, amazing and truly wonderful they are. There is much to be said of commonality – including being married – that holds friendships together. It may just be the reason why some friends decide to step away. Your true friends will stay, and others will commit to being friends with you both. It can be very sad, uncomfortable for all and compound that sense of isolation you (and your children) can feel through the process. After a while, all this fades as everyone gets used to the new normal and you may meet new friends in your post-separation circles.

Try this: If you're trying hard not to be the 'sad divorcee burden friend', give yourself a little time on the following to help you get clear on which friends can support you and how:

- Write a list of friends who you can talk to on rotation – then you don't feel guilty about dumping on just one or two! Just having this list is enough to get clear on who is there for you, and sometimes, weirdly, this can negate the necessity to phone. Call it a comfort blanket that's there when you need it.

- What are your friends' strengths? Pals don't always know how they can help, so give them jobs – like checking in on you, sending a funny meme, taking you out for a drink or inviting you to Sunday lunch (until you get your new Sunday friends for festivals, picnics and laughter), signing you up to a support group, sending 'Love you' cards in the post, or getting your ass out of bed for exercise or a walk to get some of that victim energy and cortisol (stress hormone) out of your body.

- Nominate a grounded friend or couple who still love and want to stay friends with you both to call you out if you get too 'ranty', read emails before you send them and bring you back to what matters – getting through this kindly, with as little damage as possible.

- Write these names down on a list and put it up on your fridge, or screenshot it to keep and use when you need to remember you are still loved!

Professionals

With couples choosing to have a less conflictual divorce, or a DIY divorce due to finances or choice, it would seem the divorce industry is slowly changing. Encouraging conflict for financial gain is the mindset of an old-fashioned and outdated order. It's becoming more widely recognised just how emotionally damaging divorce conflict can be on children. Many in the legal and financial professions are committed to improving their practices and understanding the emotional toll on couples as they go through the process. (Check the Resources section for links to find these professionals!)

Family lawyer

I would always recommend that if it is your intention to have a kind divorce, then you tell your lawyer at the first meeting. As much as I believe that kindness can help with everything, you need a good, word-of-mouth recommended and trusted lawyer to be on your team. I remember the shame I first felt phoning a family lawyer's office (they were great by the way – it was my sense of failure and judgement that I was carrying and the DMMs were freaking me out). However, making important decisions that are good for you is a necessary part of building your confidence for your future responsibilities as a single person or parent. Getting braver by stepping out of your emotional comfort zone and owning your divorce experience is you banking your self-empowerment. (I heard a story at a party from a lawyer bemoaning client who spend £650 an hour crying in his office… I'll leave that one with you.) Get yourself strong, prepared and empowered, especially if you don't want to pay for extra hours of your lawyer's time.

Do some of the legwork beforehand (hopefully with your Ex) to save on a lawyer's charged hours, such as organising a calendar for co-parenting, and discussing what you're going to do about pensions and where you both want to live. Don't be afraid to have these conversations, and don't commit to firm decisions until you've seen a professional to clarify, but do try to lay some of the foundations by bravely talking.

I had a friend who chose her 'bulldog' lawyer to financially spank the ass out of her husband. She wanted blood – how dare he cheat on her, embarrass, shame and reduce her to becoming a divorcee. It made no difference that for years she had been slating him while waiting for her personal trainer to make a move. She wanted to punish her husband, but she was more cross with herself that she hadn't been honest and asked for a divorce first.

Ask yourself, what are your motives in all of this? How angry are you with yourself rather than your Ex? And if you are in a place where you were blindsided and want to lash out and punish, take a moment to consider this powerful quote:

> **Holding anger is like drinking poison and waiting for the other person to die.**

Anger, conflict and punishment may provide a short-term hit of a win, but actually you want to be a long-term winner. Principle schmintziple – this stuff costs money and until you are done with being the persecutor, anger and its mates are not going to leave you.

Ask yourself:

- Does the lawyer have a matching experience and skillset to what you need? For example, do you need advice on managing trusts or assets; dealing with international elements (travel or lives connected to other countries, or offshore/non-residency issues); or balancing third-party interests (grandparents/trustees/siblings, or companies where both parties own shares)? This can be particularly important when considering lawyers who practise in multiple areas of law or where they practise in an umbrella area, such as if they have experience of working with private clients in relation to trusts but have limited experience when it comes to complex, offshore trusts. Read up on their website, see if there is a free chat available, and if it doesn't feel right or you feel there is a degree of BS involved, come back to trusting yourself. Just because you have had a free chat or a paid-for initial consultation, this doesn't mean you are obligated to use them going forward.

- Who's doing the work? If you appoint Lawyer A and their colleague Lawyer B does the work at a lower rate, are you happy with that? If Lawyer B is doing the work, are they CCing Lawyer A (who you will be paying to read each email or approve Lawyer B's drafting, and so on)? (This also applies where other 'fee earners', such as trainees and paralegals, are being copied in.)

- Are you clear on the costs? Get regular updates from your professionals. Remember, you get what you pay for – if you want a fixed-fee conveyor belt service, that's what you'll get.

- Are they someone you can work with; who you can call without feeling you're being judged? Are they a keen negotiator but also able to litigate where needed? Do they focus on what you need them to do? Do you have a good feeling and sense about them? Do they share your values? Do they clearly understand your needs, concerns and goals and are they able to work on your behalf with these in mind? Are they advising you in a way that makes you feel more knowledgeable and empowered or are they telling you what you want to hear?

It is often the case that people will instruct lawyers with similar personality traits to their own, and this may be an important consideration when finding a lawyer to assist you if, for example, you're likely to be dealing with a former partner with abusive, egotistical and/or narcissistic personality traits. While you may not want a lawyer with similar traits working with you, you may need to consider how your lawyer will deal with this.

Check out and subscribe to the *Divorce Goddess* podcast (if you haven't already discovered it) for advice on appointing a family lawyer (details provided in the Divorce Goddess link in the Resources section).

Divorce coach

A divorce coach works to support and guide you through your divorce. They have unique expertise in separation, divorce, co-parenting and the impact of divorce on children. A divorce coach will work in their own way, so finding the right person who resonates with you is key. My coaching is all about empowerment and healing because, let's face it, none of us want to walk into our future life as an emotional car crash, dragging several heavy suitcases of unresolved crap with us. A divorce coach is likely to provide you with a bespoke action plan, supportive coping strategies and resources to get you through the days where it feels like you're in a small boat in stormy seas with no safe harbour. This is when the shizzle can hit the fan – when you feel stressed, alone, vulnerable and scared.

Typically, divorce coaches cover:

- How you tell your spouse you want a divorce
- Recommending legal, financial and therapeutic professionals to support you
- Assisting with completing divorce documentation
- A plan and tool kit to manage divorce emotions, including stress and fear

- Preparing and telling your children
- Managing a difficult Ex, stopping being triggered and building resilience
- Preparing mentally and emotionally for meetings or mediation
- Effective co-parenting, with strategies to support you all moving forwards with less conflict
- Dating with confidence and learning how to trust again
- Self-development, empowerment and future planning

Coaches actively encourage and support you to step outside your comfort zone, do the work on your self-development and say yes to yourself so you feel empowered to take action, grow into the new you, and feel more confident and hopeful about your future life!

Kinder divorces don't happen on their own – they happen when you do the work and invest in yourself. Asking for help is one of the most powerful things you can do.

My client Meera kindly wrote: "I feel so lucky to have spoken to Tosh when I did; my relationship with my Ex was at a pivotal point. Not only did she introduce a new way of acting towards my

Ex, but she taught me that it's okay to show kindness and compassion at a time like this. If someone said I would be in this place, after my husband left me when I was seven months pregnant, I would have laughed in their face – but it's actually happened!! After months of overthinking and having this battle in my head of how to 'win', what to say, how to act, etc., Tosh helped me to see sense and to just concentrate on 'nourishing my own backyard'. I'm now better able to live in the present moment, I'm learning to work with those horrible feelings (that creep up on you at 3am) and best of all, I'm starting to feel nuggets of self-love, which is helping to mend my broken heart. I'm now able to just focus on my beautiful baby boy and rock my new role of being an amazing single mum!"

Mediation

Mediation is the process by which you both sit down with a neutral third party (a mediator) who supports and guides you to work through, negotiate and resolve issues, such as a financial settlement or co-parenting agreement. Mediators can be family lawyers or other professionals who have undergone family mediation training. As with the other professionals mentioned, do take time to get referrals, do your research and trust in the process.

The mediation process worked for me and my Ex. Honestly, we were done with the fighting, we were running out of funds fast, and we needed to make some big decisions inexpensively. In short, we had to find a way out of the carnage as financially and emotionally intact as we could. If you can leave your ego at the door, and commit to kindness over conflict, then mediation is a route absolutely worth exploring.

Shuttle mediation is also available to couples, which facilitates the mediation process without you having to see or hear your Ex, and if it is suitable, you can also mediate online.

To find a local mediator, turn to the Professional Resources in the Resources section, where you will also find a link to my *Divorce Goddess* podcast (check out the episode where I talk to my own mediator about mediation).

Financial advisors and planners

Never underestimate the importance of getting on top of your finances, diminished amounts of money or not. Getting a plan of action for your divorce settlement and future will not only help you sleep better, but you'll know where you are, rather than stumbling on fearing destitution and going through your divorce anxious, scared and in battle.

Sometimes you have to invest in yourself to literally invest in yourself!

If you're in debt or fretting about money and feeling stuck, ask around – do any of your friends have a financial advisor they trust and could recommend? Is there a family member who is good with money that you can ask for support or advice? Remember, people love to help!

If you've not had a handle on your marital finances, know this:

There's no shame in asking for help with the stuff you don't know about.

A client brought to a session some red-marked envelopes that made her feel sick every day. She couldn't bring herself to open them, felt so ashamed and found it increasingly difficult to face the reality of her financial situation. We went through them together, called a financial charity and, in a couple of hours, this whole heavy burden had left her. This time was also her saying 'yes' to herself by applying self-kindness, and she gained the confidence to get to grips with her future finances.

Get over yourself, swallow your pride and ASK… you owe this great self-kindness to yourself. And if you need a helping hand, call on a friend, grab a coffee and reach out with them right beside you.

Susie said: "I cannot tell you how scary it was to go through a divorce as a stay-at-home mum, having given up a career to be faced at 55 years of age with financial uncertainty. I never thought I would be asking questions at this time in my life like, "Where am I going to live?", "What is going to happen to me?", "What will I do without a pension?" It was a living nightmare for me. I found meditation to settle my anxiety but I also needed to get advice and I'd advise anyone to find a good professional as soon as possible to give you guidance, a better night's sleep and hope for your future."

When you're choosing a financial planner/advisor, consider if they:

- Are free from conflict of interests – they must have your interests as their client in the forefront of their minds
- Are experienced – markets move up and down, laws change, economies grow and slump, so choose someone who has personally witnessed these events and can guide you through them with wisdom
- Share your values – this is about rapport, trust and liveability, but fundamentally you want to ensure that they see the world the same as you
- Are ready to work with you over the long term – you should make the selection based on a whole lifetime together

- Have been referred from a trusted source – if someone else has vouched for them (or indeed several people have) then this is a very good place to start (especially if they also share your values!)

Try this: Download my Managing Difficulties meditation for a confidence boost to settle your DMMs if you have some hard decisions to make regarding finances (go to the Divorce Goddess link in the Resources section).

The Resources section has links to charities who can offer advice, plus information about regulated financial professionals (under Professional Resources). My Instagram page (@divorcegoddess) is also full of professionals I am happy to recommend and introduce.

Therapists

I'm a big fan of therapy, no matter what you're going through. If you need to talk, get a massage or energy healing, then this is where I'm all in. If you don't know what to do next, head towards self-kindness and therapy, please!

I initially went to therapy because I needed help letting go of my emotions that were causing me no end of stress pain in my tummy (DMMs screamed "ulcer"… it wasn't). This was also the time I started my blog (see the Divorce Goddess link in the Resources section), which was incredibly cathartic for me as I felt better for writing about how I felt, plus my experiences seemed to be helping others (100k reads!) so I felt good about that too. If you've never tried any therapy or see it as something for people who 'aren't strong enough', I challenge you to give it a go, get out of your comfort zone and ask yourself, "What have I got to lose?" A therapist will listen to you, and encourage you to release some of the emotional turmoil inside you with a kind, non-judgemental ear. You may fancy energy healing or having your muscles worked on to release tension – please make the call!

You may want to seek out a therapist who has been divorced themselves (if you're wanting to talk to a counsellor or psychotherapist) or you may not, it is up to you – we are all different, but it may be something you want to consider.

Please do not be afraid to explore different dispute options like the ones explored in this chapter, and take time to find out more about the divorce process so you can both look at project-managing your way out of this together. Surely you'd rather you had a say, than a court system and a stranger deciding what happens with your finances or children. As with every life experience, don't forget:

Knowledge is power

and if doing some research gets you a better night's sleep through the divorce days because you feel more in control and knowledgeable about what's happening, rather than going through it blindly, just do it. Kindness for conflict is about finding balance, doing your own research and having the courage to ask for help. Know that you can dig deep to find the confidence to ask important questions, and do not be afraid to do your due diligence on your potential professionals, as you would with a tradesperson or a medical professional. Yes, this is a form of self-kindness as it builds your confidence muscles going forwards.

Using trusted professionals works to get you all through the divorce process without so much conflict. Having children binds you for many, many years (think future events such as births, deaths and marriages). Knowing that everything has been ironed out saves unnecessary future pain and the potential breaking down of co-parenting relationships moving forward.

Professionals are there to help and support you; they know what you don't. If you want to feel more empowered and own your divorce confidently, step off that ledge of fear, and begin trusting that you will learn to fly.

Finally

If you're not feeling so much love for yourself based upon what is happening or has happened, I cannot tell you enough how important it is to begin practising self-kindness, like right now! Whether you are consumed with guilt for calling time on your relationship and hating yourself for inflicting pain on those you love, or you feel unloved and worthless due to your spouse moving on or finding someone else, it is time to do this self-love/self-kindness thing!

Self-kindness is the balm to helping you manage these difficult, self-judging and unkind thoughts. You are not your thoughts, no matter how much the DMMs want you to believe them. Each time you practise self-kindness, you are saying yes to yourself rather than the DMMs; saying yes to you helps you grow your self-confidence, regain your self-worth and you begin to reconnect back to the important you.

Our relationship with ourselves reflects our relationship with others.

Words are powerful. We all know this – they inflict pain, suffering and they can change lives in an instant. They can also change how we feel about ourselves. In the following exercise, I am going to ask you to do something pretty powerful and although it may feel a bit out of your comfort zone, I really want you to find the courage to do this.

Try this: This is literally a must for all my clients and is a game-changer for those who take the plunge:

- Message all those that love you and ask them to describe you in three positive words.
- Keep a note of the words and then write a list of the top six.
- Notice how you feel and how your body responds to these words... Perhaps your body feels lighter, tingly and relaxed?
- How have these six words changed your mood?
- How can you use these words to change your thoughts?

Write them down everywhere – mood boards, bathroom mirror, fridge door – and READ them when you have those moments where you forget exactly how strong and amazing you are. You can also say them to yourself each day as a mantra: "I am..." It may feel a little uncomfortable at first, so check in to see how these words change how you feel or adjust your energy after repeating them. For a self-power-up, try saying them to yourself while looking in the mirror!

Alice said, "I was a bit apprehensive about doing this and initially also felt it was a bit self-indulgent. But I actually really enjoyed it and my friends and family have made me feel really good today –

it put a smile on my face and some friends have asked me what I think of them in return! I'd recommend people do this no matter what! The words that came out on top for me were: independent, intelligent, strong and fun/funny! These are all things that I know I have been, but I haven't felt those things in a while. There were some others that made me laugh, like 'vivacious'."

Now you have a better idea of just how much of a great human you are in others' eyes, it is time to see this yourself. Notice the words you use about yourself throughout the day – especially when things aren't going so well, or you are triggered or wake up feeling 'divorce blue'. Do you go into negative self-talk or are you there for yourself? As you become more aware of the words you use about yourself and others, you can choose not to use them. Dropping into my 'woo woo' bit for a moment – words have an energy, and if you are not sure what I mean by that, notice how you feel after a 'bitchin' negative session rather than a happy positive one.

In the next chapter, we will be diving into hope, a feeling that if we cultivate it, it stays… just like you with this process!

Chapter 2

Hope

HOPE is seeing those beautiful life moments that shine brighter on the darkest divorce days.

You picked up this book because you were either curious, divorce-conflict exhausted, or something inside you felt good when you read the title. While writing this book, I learned that Hope comes from Opportunities that present themselves to People, who if they take them, are more likely to feel Empowered. Maybe this book is your opportunity?

Whatever spoke to you, trust it. It's those moments of clarity that appear when we're less present in our lives, and these in turn lead us to feeling more confident so we can make wiser, calmer and kinder decisions, no matter what conflict we're dealing with in life.

There is always hope – sometimes we need to trust that if one door is closed to us, then there's another one open somewhere, ready for us to walk through. Hope comes when we stop to listen, feel into and be with what is happening so we can stop all the 'doing' and instead spend more time 'being' (check back to the Introduction to refresh yourself about automatic pilot mode if you need to). We're then able to experience a new way of living; a more conscious, kinder and less conflictual way, which is then reflected in our divorce experience. Taking a less travelled path is going to introduce you to the unknown, ask you to dig deeper and teach you to live a little differently, which may or may not challenge you.

Hope is realising your divorce is an opportunity and that you don't always have to be triggered by your Ex and end up in conflict. It is in your children's eyes as they see you together, being amicable as co-parents. It is the ability to find those glimmers of light you collect along the way for the tougher days.

In this chapter, we'll continue to build on the self-kindness foundations of Chapter 1 and begin to incorporate hopeful new ways of thinking into the following areas:

- Doing divorce differently by changing the way you think about your divorce
- Changing the way you see your relationship with your Ex as you build a new relationship with them

- Stopping yourself from committing 'social media murder' and going 'pain hunting'
- Using the '5Ps' to manage difficulties around meetings, conversations and pick-ups/drop-offs
- Managing finance fears in a different way that saves you money
- Rethinking home – when there is love in your heart, it doesn't matter where you live

Doing Divorce Differently

If you want to cultivate hope and see a better, kinder outcome to your divorce, the kicker is that you have to put yourself out of your comfort zone and do things differently. Choosing to divorce differently is a leap of faith – firstly for yourself and those you love, and secondly for your Ex.

Doing things differently is all about creating new neural pathways. Think of a park in summer – the paths are really worn and there are stretches of greener, unwalked-upon grass in between. I invite you to see a kinder divorce as you choose to walk a new path across untouched green grass.

Take a moment to notice how you feel about walking this new path (if it helps, take yourself into a park in your head – or a real park! – and see yourself walking your new path across the grass).

Be aware of how you're feeling as you cross this fresh grass. The divorce mind monkeys (DMMs) hate 'different'; they resist greatly because they want to keep you safe. Maybe you notice the DMMs shouting "Keep off the grass!" and telling you it's fraught with unexpected danger? These are your thoughts, not necessarily your reality.

Doing everyday tasks a little differently allows you to build future resilience and better manage the unexpected bumps in the divorce road. You take back control from your DMMs. When you step out of your comfort zone and realise you're okay, your confidence grows and you feel empowered.

Doing things differently during your divorce doesn't have to be difficult. It may be challenging, like anything that moves you forward, but the purpose is to make life easier for you and your Ex in the long run – with less conflict, less regret and minimal emotional fallout.

Try this: Experiment with doing things differently in different parts of your everyday life:

- **Timekeeping:** Change from being late all the time to being an on-time person.
- **Cooking:** If you're not a great chef, learn to cook! If you are a great chef, try a new recipe!

- **Language:** Avoid using trigger words (the ones that get your Ex riled); instead, learn some new positive ones.
- **Stress management:** Minimise stress by adopting some calming practices, like meditation or breathing exercises.
- **DIY:** Learn some basic DIY skills so you can be self-reliant.
- **Finances:** If you're not financially savvy, get on it, be brave and learn to work out the figures! (Chapter 1 has more on finding help with finances in the 'Financial advisors and planners' section.)
- **Planning and organisation:** Use checklists to make sure the kids go to stay with your Ex with everything they need.

Looking at what isn't working, getting out of your comfort zone and making changes to how you live your life can be powerful. I personally think our comfort zone is actually our discomfort zone. Why? Because it is the place that we are scared to leave and where we stay small.

Your comfort zone + Fear (of leaving it) = Your discomfort zone

Divorce sticks dynamite in comfort zones. It helps you realise that life's perceived comfort or 'safe' zone is really your discomfort zone – but you can turn your discomfort zone into a real comfort zone by finding the courage to try things differently:

Your discomfort zone + Courage = Your real comfort zone (where the magic happens!)

Courage gives you the confidence to venture into unknown places, meet new friends and realise that you're still alive, you're okay and, importantly, you're in a place where you say YES to yourself. As you begin to do things differently, you begin to lean into the possibilities of being in your real comfort zone and seeing the potential of everything available to you through and after your divorce. *This* is where life's magic happens.

A client, Sarah, said her life was in a permanent state of "petrification". Her whole safe world imploded on discovering her husband's affair. When I told her about the comfort/discomfort zones, she said that she realised how insular her world had become, and how reliant she had been on her husband to support her when travelling, socialising and even clothes shopping. She had very little confidence, so we worked with doing things differently each week until finally she felt more confident. The week after she received her Decree Absolute she got on a plane and walked the Annapurna Trail in Nepal with a group of people she'd never met before. Looking back at her life, she couldn't believe it took a divorce to do something like this, and said, "I've never looked back!"

Try this: Start with small and easy tasks to notice how you feel as you get out of your comfort zone and grow your 'brave' muscle:

- Walk a different route to work or the shops
- Go round a supermarket the opposite way
- Buy and cook different foods
- Start using different words about yourself
- Shower after breakfast instead of before
- Make time to be kind to yourself
- Wear a different coloured T-shirt/jumper (or buy some red underwear – I dare you!)
- Buy a new style of book – and make time to read it
- Learn a new language
- Attend a yoga class

With each small change, be present with what you're doing, notice how it makes you feel and be with those feelings – don't try to run away from them, and note that the sky didn't fall on you afterwards (thank you, Chicken Licken).

Doing something in a different way can be scary – it can rouse the DMMs from their slumber and test your boundaries. But doing things differently is a worthwhile recalibration of your life. It can help take you off automatic pilot and put you into the present moment, focusing on what you're actually doing rather than being stuck and scared in your divorce-exhausted head. As Susan Jeffers famously said (in her book of the same name), "Feel the fear and do it anyway."

Doing things differently also grows your resilience. You're less likely to be triggered by a difficult Ex or life's bumps in the road (which you can then deal with more calmly), and you can look after yourself better when you're not in a permanent state of 'triggeration' (so tiring!).

Try this: In times when you're feeling overwhelmed, your mind is racing or you're feeling stressed (perhaps before a call or a pick-up/drop-off), practise this simple STOP exercise:

- Set your phone alarm to go off at two-hourly intervals during the day.
- Take a minute to STOP:

- S = Stop
- T = Take a breath
- O = Observe
- P = Proceed

- STOP what you're doing.
- TAKE a deep breath down into your belly, following your breath with your mind.
- OBSERVE how you're feeling – take another deep breath. Perhaps irritated, rushed or impatient ("I'm in the middle of making supper" or "I'm trying to sort the washing out" – the glam of single life!). If you're stressed, what can you do to help yourself? For example, drink some water, eat something, go for a walk, rest?
- PROCEED with what you're doing – feeling calmer, less anxious and more aware.

Notice how you feel afterwards. This exercise helps you stop your DMMs from focusing on repetitive, challenging thoughts that may be whirring around noisily in your head – think of it as a mini thought reset.

Your Relationship with Your Ex

Divorce grief is not to be underestimated – it is big, it is sneaky and it is painful. Pain clouds our ability to remember clearly, which gives the grief monkeys an opportunity to come out with their rose-tinted specs on and repeatedly wrongfoot you. It's so easy to lose perspective on what your relationship really was – the good, the bad and the downright ugly bits.

Your Ex is your Ex for a reason. It may not be a reason that you felt you had any choice over – maybe your hand was forced and you feel wronged, negative, angry, ashamed, guilty… the list can go on – but what's important when moving forward in a divorce is that you try to balance out the negative with the positive, especially if you have children.

Hopes are dashed at the end of a relationship. Everything can feel mightily unfair and sad, and the feeling of failure can weigh heavy. But there is hope to be found, and a chance to lay the foundations for a different (and more hopeful) relationship with your Ex as you move forwards with your lives.

In this section I invite you to take an overview of the different parts of your relationship: to look at the parts that you will and will NOT miss – as well as to think about what your future relationship with your Ex might look like.

Try this: Here are some areas to think about – with some examples to get you started that may ring true for you (or not):

- I WILL MISS… another adult in the house, my home, help with the kids, my Ex's parents, a cup of tea made for me on a Sunday morning, someone to have a glass of wine with on the sofa, the dog, physical contact

- I WON'T MISS… the conflict, the untidiness, their emotional unavailability, their grumpiness, having to go on holiday with my Ex rather than a friend, being ignored, the dog, walking around on eggshells, physical contact

- THREE THINGS THAT I APPRECIATE ABOUT MY EX… (I know, I know!! But go for it, even if you have to dig deep…) they pay maintenance, they are a good parent, they don't want conflict, this experience has given me some life lessons

- THREE THINGS THAT MY EX APPRECIATES ABOUT ME… I am organised about school emails/trips/school clubs, I will check a tyre or mow the lawn, I'll suggest meal ideas for the children, I'll help to put their new place together or do occasional DIY (to support the children's living space), we attend parent/teacher meetings together, I keep to timings and agreements

Consider this scenario: You spend your free weekend worrying about what your children are eating at your Ex's house, especially if they are a terrible cook or hate cooking. Ask yourself, "What can I do to support them so they can parent our children better?" Perhaps you could teach your Ex and your kids – especially if they are teens – a couple of easy, tried-and-tested recipes? Better still, why don't you give yourself – and them – a break and let it go, trusting that all will be okay?

If you have kids, you will be inextricably linked for some time. If your children are going to benefit, changing your thoughts around your Ex can ultimately soften the experience. When the kids see you both working together, it is a gift to them because they can see that something good can come out of something bad. It can certainly help allay any of the DMM guilt you may have for past regrets.

Working with your Ex is about continually moving forwards and noticing the good stuff too – such as when you both have positive moments together (sharing an inside joke, talking about the children, talking about the in-laws, being friendly at pick-ups/drop-offs, making co-parenting decisions…).

Life doesn't need to be difficult and stressful… with a little kindness, the possibilities are endless.

Try this: You may also want to consider the following questions as you begin the process of moving forward in a new way:

- WHAT ARE YOUR FUTURE FRIENDSHIP GOALS? Co-parenting on friendly terms for the kids' sakes; being able to attend future life events alongside each other (such as birthdays, weddings and funerals); accepting new partners.

- HOW CAN I BE MORE OPEN-MINDED AND ACCEPTING OF MY EX? Picking your battles; letting go of the small stuff; lateness/disorganisation (they might never change – with this, better the devil you know).

- WHAT ARE YOUR EX'S GOALS AND ARE YOU ABLE TO SUPPORT THEM? Helping them with childcare so they can work; encouraging them to go for a promotion or to start back at work; being more flexible if they want to start a business.

Kindness rather than conflict is good for the mental and emotional wellbeing of you both, and those you love.

Andrew (48) came to see me after his long-term partner left him. He still loved her, and he needed help to come to terms with letting her go so he could begin to move on. We worked with a kinder approach rather than punishing her, and at the end of the first session he said, "Through this separation I want to be a gentleman," which was music to the kindness ears! He said he felt better with this approach, less stressed about being unkind to the mum of his two children and kinder towards himself. As he said, "Sometimes we just need to know that there is another way and have the courage to try it."

It is in these moments of wisdom, as you become aware of how you feel when applying kindness – even in the most challenging of circumstances – that I believe the magic in life happens. Having the courage to do something different and with kindness, in the most extreme circumstances, is like banking karma (karma is what happens to you as a result of your actions – think putting out the good stuff and it coming back to you).

I believe that the karma bank starts working for you when you do things from a place of genuine, authentic kindness and love. If you're thinking in a manipulative way about your Ex and you do something to get something back, the law of karma is going to run a mile. Instead, aim to do something good without any expectation of it coming back to you and see what happens.

Changing how we respond to the triggers that make us see all-out red (which sets off the DMMs) comes with practice, effort and consistency. What I mean by *responding* is this – you come from a place of calmness, wisdom and thought as opposed to *reacting* (which is automatic, and comes from learned habits of behaviour that can result in regret, guilt and shame). Adopting small habits each day helps you grow your awareness and develop your experience of the 'now' moment, so you can see when you're heading into conflict (reacting) rather than kindness (responding). The more work you do to let go of anger and reduce conflict, the better you're going to feel, and this comes with becoming more conscious of your thoughts, words and actions.

Try this: Breathe in deeply and say to yourself, "I breathe in calm." Exhale and say to yourself, "I breathe out anger" (you might want to use alternative words that feel right for you). Do this several times.

Check in with your body when you feel yourself heading down 'Conflict Alley – are your muscles tense; do you have a rock in your belly; are you holding your breath, or something else? Does it feel good to be in a heightened state of fight, flight or freeze mode (explained in the Introduction)? Noticing these bodily sensations helps you get better at choosing a kinder route, so think of them as your inbuilt sat nav alerts. How would it feel to be able to minimise the dread of seeing or speaking to your Ex? How much more relaxing would that be – what a relief!? Checking in with your body and how that feels is your best barometer as to what is working for you and what isn't.

Generally, when you're reframing your relationship with your Ex, it's good to remember:

- Your Ex doesn't need to do anything for you emotionally anymore. For the kids, yes, but not for you. If you're expecting emotional support from your Ex on your wobbly days, phone a friend instead – and don't seek support from your children either. It's hard getting out of the habit of turning to your Ex, so see your updated support network as a necessary part of the process of letting go and moving on. Try journaling how you feel, doing some exercise and looking at how you can make more time for better self-care.

- If your Ex has narcissistic tendencies or is difficult, make it your mission to get better at emotional 'flatlining' around those potential hotspots – think water off a duck's back! Get better with your boundaries so you don't feed into their narrative. Expecting an Ex with narcissistic tendencies to change, especially during or after divorce, is literally you haemorrhaging your energy. Learning to emotionally disconnect and changing how you react to your Ex is, in truth, the kindest thing you can do for yourself. Keep your energy for you! (More on this in Chapter 6, in the section 'Staying in Your Own Backyard: Keeping Your Energy for You'.)

- Keep your conversations functional and emotionless – which can be hard, as they're likely to be emotionally charged conversations. This is dangerous territory, as the DMMs will try to wade in, which could be a one-way street that takes you backwards rather than forwards. The phrase "bite your lip" may be helpful here (I love the old nuggets of advice!). And if you don't want to speak and would prefer to email or message (maybe because you're feeling wobbly, tearful or angry), then let them know this is the reason why you're choosing this form of communication. By being a little bit vulnerable, you're honouring yourself and speaking your truth rather than making it about what your Ex thinks. You've got to stop caring about what they think and come back to trusting you can do this on your own.

What I found helpful after feeling challenged on every level being on my own was this: the more I got into the mindset that I had my own back, the less I needed to find emotional support from my Ex.

Holding on to your Ex as an emotional lifeline is delaying the inevitable. It makes space for the DMMs to create trouble and strife and you'll find you take those unwanted steps backwards, leading to a greater sense of frustration and failure. The more you practise standing in your own power, the easier it will be to apply kindness to conflict and manage emotionally on your own.

Try this: Get good at checking in with your emotions before you speak to your Ex. Make it a habit to repeat a phrase or mantra to get yourself into a more positive space.

I used this mantra when I was triggered: "You will not have my anger."

You are here to move forwards, not backwards. You can do this and, yes – you are strong.

Here are some other mantras I've used and recommended to clients:

- "I am powerful, I can do hard things and I have my own back always."
- "I live every day knowing that happiness is within me and part of who I am."
- "I am connected to my truth, I am living authentically, and I come from a place of forgiveness and innerstanding."

- "I listen to my body and nourish it with love and kindness."
- "I communicate compassionately, knowing I am enough and I can do this."
- "I know I am bigger than what my Ex thinks of me."

Walking the Talk: Social Media Murder and Pain Hunting

Hope comes from investing in yourself and growing your confidence – and this comes from increasing your awareness around what nourishes you and what depletes you. When you consciously choose not to drop into unhelpful habits or addictions, you say yes to yourself. You begin to gather glimmers of hope that you're strong enough to do this hard stuff. Resistance isn't futile – use it as a tool to identify what isn't working for you and empower yourself to take more positive actions. Resistance can open the doorway to hope.

So… let's talk social media – a curse and a blessing for us all in this modern world. By 'social media murder' and 'pain hunting', I mean trawling social media late at night (whether under the influence of alcohol or not) to play imaginary Cluedo with your Ex (and maybe their new partner), and checking what they're up to and who they're spending time with (old mutual friends). This is an invitation to 'murder' your weekend happiness, so I urge you to resist – why torment yourself?

The DMMs love comparison and thrive on FOMO – fear of missing out, which I talk about more in Chapter 3 in the section 'Let's talk FOMO (the crippling Fear of Missing Out)'. Nothing makes us feel the loneliness, hear the 'I'm not good enough' story or experience the lack-of-self-worth jitters more than those apps twinkling their merry 'let's f*ck with your head and heart' notifications on a Friday night.

Consider Katherine's story. Does this sound familiar to you?

"I couldn't stop myself on those Friday nights after my Ex had picked up the kids. I would sit down with a bottle of wine – the next thing I knew, my phone would beep with a notification and that would be it... I'd disappear down that rabbit hole, tormenting, emotionally stabbing and comparing myself. I'd then trawl through mutual friends' accounts to find my Ex, see what he was doing and with whom, and I would spend the rest of the weekend angry, resentful and alone. It was addictive and it compounded my sense of worthlessness, failure and loneliness, and I hated myself even more for putting myself through it."

Katherine's story is not a one-off. She'd fallen into this habit instead of enjoying her weekend off. She knew that it was going to hurt her, but she still did it to herself. We put together a plan for her to use so she could manage those tormenting DMMs, which were urging her to be unkind to herself; she found new friends, deleted the app for a couple of months and felt like she was enjoying her free weekends again without this negative, damaging and confidence-shredding habit eating away at her.

Resisting the pull of social media

We have a choice every time whether we react or respond. We also have the choice to forgive ourselves for going down that social media rabbit hole. It's a bit like reaching for the beer, wine or gin – what is it that makes you reach for the booze rather than thinking "this isn't going to serve me or help me sleep", especially if you have an important meeting the next day? Self-sabotage is often a feature of the divorce process. Following the guidance in this book and putting together a toolkit of practices you can use to become more self-aware gives you the choice to walk away from self-sabotage.

The conflict we hold within ourselves that comes from regret, disappointment and anger can sit loudly inside us during times when we're alone or lonely. A quiet weekend may be when the mess gets messier and you're caught in the middle of it, not knowing how to get out. We're far more likely to sabotage a potentially good evening when we choose social media over our own peace.

As William Shakespeare so eloquently wrote in *The Tempest*, "Hell is empty and all the devils are here."

It reminds me of the two arrows story (which I first heard from my wonderful mindfulness teacher trainer, Shamash Alidina). The first arrow is the event that hurts us (such as knowing that your Ex is at a party of old mutual friends and who post their party photos on social media). The second arrow is what you choose to do with the knowledge – do you wound yourself again with the second arrow because you go looking ('pain hunting'), or do you choose not to look and put the second arrow down? In essence, what you do with the second arrow is optional. (When I first heard this story, it made so much sense that I got two arrows tattooed on my wrists to remind me.) You get to empower yourself by choosing kind or conflictual social media behaviours.

'Walking the talk' with kindness in divorce is about times like those weekends when you're faced with what one client described as "family hell". You stick your nose out of your front door and perceive that every family or couple is happy and together, and it hurts – even though the reality is that they may also have challenging stuff going on. The temptation can be too great to really stick the knife into yourself by checking out the happy, successful families posting selfies of enjoying life on the ski slopes, on the beach or with once-mutual friends. You may as well order in extra salt and not just rub but *scrub* it into your wounds!

Fortunately, you can choose social media behaviours that serve you well rather than hurt like hell.

Try this: It's all about adopting new, more positive habits around those parts of our lives that hurt the most:

- Unfollow or mute the friends and family lives that most upset you.
- Take off those unhelpful notifications in your settings – like, seriously!
- Unfriend and block your Ex, their new partner (if this applies) and anyone connected to them (better still, download an app that blocks social media for you).
- If the thought comes up over the weekend to go pain hunting, ask yourself: "Do I need this on top of everything else? Is it helpful for me to see this stuff – is this self-kindness?" (Have a friend who you can call for this specific reason who will NOT judge you, but will instead call you out.)
- Identify those times during the weekend when you're most likely to 'social media murder' your confidence and self-worth, and during these times choose to turn off your phone, leave it on flight mode or put it in another room. If your phone needs to stay on, take a moment, at this edge of unreasonable and damaging behaviour, to take a deep breath and purposefully have a chat with yourself. Why do you want to hurt yourself? What benefit will this bring

you? Do you need to do this? Do something else instead, like ten star jumps, a kitchen dance, put your trainers on and take the dog for a walk, bite a lemon… do anything that takes the DMMs out of your ear, whispering that this could be a good idea!

Remember: comparison is a mean thief of your joy and confidence!

If you want to enjoy a glass or two of your favourite sauce at the weekend, try not to think about posting comments, unkind remarks or obvious digs on accounts that are going to get back to your Ex. Is this conducive to a kinder approach or will it increase conflict? Erm… leaving this with you...

Remember: you are bigger than the sum of a few words on a social media post, no matter what or how you are feeling – so resist!

The more you resist, the less opportunities the DMMs have to encourage you to take this particular pain pathway. You have a choice... you do NOT have to pick up that second arrow and hurt yourself.

Rising above social media storytelling

I was asked a question by one of my Instagram followers about what to do when your Ex is telling everyone a different story about what happened – including, sadly, your own family.

Why do you think they might be shouting the loudest? Could it be because they KNOW they're in the wrong or at fault on some level, and they're scared of what others are going to think if they find out? Or might it be because they are in fact the person they're describing you to be, and so they're using their own behaviours and actions to stay in avoidance mode?

Either way, take it as a win when your Ex (or anyone else) feels the need to talk about you and share their story. This is their stuff, not yours. Take a step back, observe the situation and hold your power by waiting for those that really care and love you to ask you what really happened.

If, after a week of divorce hell, you feel tempted to wade in and 'set the record straight' so everyone knows the truth, remember this:

You do not have to wade in!

Shaming is a low-grade form of trying to make your actions, words and thoughts acceptable to everyone else, except the shaming is on you (that's the kicker, right?!). Where your thoughts and words go, your energy flows. It's like watching depressing news – you may feel your mood has dropped, and this can happen with us and our own words. The 14th-century Persian poet Hafez asks you to look at the house you're living in by the words you build the walls with. What sort of house do you want to live in – one that is positive and empowered or one that feels low-energy and heavy? So, if you notice you're on a bitchin' roll after a particularly shocking week, make a conscious decision to stop adding to the negativity.

Try reducing the depth of this unhelpful neural pathway or creating a new one (remember the path over the green grass that you can choose to create by doing divorce differently?) by not posting negative comments or rants on social media. No one (including you) wants to hear the hate talk on a night out, either. Ask yourself honestly, "Do I need to do this – do I need to spoil the gift of a night out with divorce toxicity?"

The more you grow the habit of stopping yourself from rising to the bait, the less you'll do it. Trust me: you'll feel better for it.

A client once asked me if the anger and toxicity would stay inside them if they didn't talk about it, which is a great question! Acknowledge the anger then consciously choose an alternative outlet for it, which is why journaling, marching up big hills, training for an ironman, therapy, counselling, coaching – whatever it takes – can help you turn anger into self-empowerment. Create this new habit and instead talk about the positive things you want to do – maybe this is the time to start a new hobby, redecorate your bedroom or set up your own business!

Try this: If you need to release some anger verbally, reach for your list of people to call on (those in your support squad – refer to the section on 'Friends' in 'Rallying Your Support Squad' in Chapter 1) and keep the ranting with them... or work with a therapist or coach.

Hope for a better future happens when you sow kinder seeds every time you hold your grace, dignity and power by not shaming, gossiping and complaining about your Ex. Stop watering the conflict and start feeling those 'hope feels'!

If you need to, surround yourself with new people – you can use your social media positively for that!

Managing Difficulties – the Divorce 5Ps

A fellow divorcee once said to me that divorce life is "relentless". Like everything, if it's not working well for you, things need to change! You may need to get more organised, manage your difficulties more effectively and come back to focusing on hope.

If your intention is to have a kinder, more mindful divorce with less conflict, then emotional, mental, spiritual and physical self-care is the way to go! I cannot emphasise enough how exercising self-kindness can improve your experience of your divorce and minimise conflict.

Areas that create A LOT of stress for people experiencing divorce, in no particular order, include worries about:

- Being alone forever
- Being poverty-stricken
- Not being able to see your children
- Being a bad, guilt-ridden parent
- Selling your home and having nowhere to live
- Being friendless and not having support
- Feeling emotionally scarred for life

Being aware of the DMMs' ability to mess with your head on an alarmingly regular basis is the key to managing your difficulties more effectively and reducing your stress levels. You feel more in control, your Ex gets less frustrated, and the children will be less affected by potential conflict.

The divorce 5Ps are:

Prior Preparation Prevents Poor Performance

The 5Ps were my go-to when I was managing stressful areas through my divorce. Weirdly, the 5Ps came from my Ex and his approach to life – it's a nugget that has stuck with me, and I thank him for that as it has become one of the pillars of my divorce coaching practice.

The 5Ps are especially helpful when preparing for those flash points in life: the meetings that make you want to throw up in fear; the introduction of new partners; filling in the divorce paperwork; facing the playground parents; telling family; first dates with someone new… They're also helpful when you know you're going to see your Ex in more everyday ways, such as during pick-ups and drop-offs.

Whatever you're dealing with that isn't working or where you feel you're not making progress, try and apply the 5Ps.

PRIOR

I'm calling out those of you who can't even say hello to your Ex without a snarky smile or a grimacey 'f**k you' look. Just start practising saying "hello" and a genuine "how are you?" to yourself in the mirror, or imagine saying it to them. The more you get comfortable doing this, the more that new neural pathway will develop.

If you're a parent then this really is a must – there are going to be many hellos, including in front of your children!

Try this: Keep these tips in mind if you need to get your headspace right prior to seeing your Ex:

- Give yourself permission to let go of the small stuff that the DMMs have been niggling at you about. Choose your battles (I hate saying this but it works here), and if it feels right, it is right. For example, try not to get triggered by lateness if it is occasional.

- Notice when the DMMs challenge you (maybe because a friend had a similar experience that wasn't so great). This is your divorce, not theirs, so keep coming back to your Divorce Intention (refer to the section 'The Beginning: Setting Your Intention' in Chapter 1). This is an opportunity to check in with your Intention, and remind yourself of what you want to commit to and where you want to be heading.

- Be proactive in your approach. For example, if you're worried about asking a question about, say, finances for fear of being judged or looking stupid, remember this whole process is important and your questions matter – don't wait until it is too late to generate a positive outcome (such as clarifying weekend plans for the children or a financial situation).

- Make a list of the trigger words you use that are going to inflame your Ex, and greatly resist using them. Recognise your defensive body language (such as having your arms crossed) and again be more aware if you do this so you can stop. Get good at checking in with yourself to consciously make small adjustments so you're better able to manage that reactive rather than responsive habit.

- Commit to being friendly. I'm always guided back to the possibility that you can be a bigger person, leave your ego at the door and put in the extra effort. If it's not reciprocated, at least you know you did better – PLUS, remember your Ex is still the other parent if you have children.

PREPARATION

This P is absolutely within your control, and down to you and you only. Here are some simple ways you can prepare yourself with a little self-care:

- Try to get to bed early; and if you haven't slept well, check in with yourself before the event. It's normal to feel sad, unfulfilled, anxious, exhausted, unsure or overwhelmed with little or no sleep. Give yourself permission to feel whatever you're feeling. Just notice any patterns so you can keep a check on yourself (this is you having your own back!).

- Choose not to drink coffee or sugary, stimulant-fuelled drinks that make you feel hyper or anxious – instead, go for a caffeine-free tea or drink water. Remember to eat beforehand too to avoid getting 'hangry' – a prescription for self-kindness rather than conflict.

- Get your meditation practice working for you with a short meditation before you meet, such as five deep breaths (in for four, out for six) down into your belly (which you can do in the car, on the bus or even in the loo!). Never ever did I think a public toilet would become a safe haven where I would be able to take a few deep breaths and feel calmer (who knew!). Take those deep breaths into your belly and trigger your body's natural relaxation response!

- Do some exercise beforehand to get that excess energy out of your system! Try a run, a walk in nature, stretching, yoga – leaving less for the DMMs to feed off. Get yourself to where you need to be early, walk around rather than scrolling social media, and focus your thoughts on what is actually happening rather than what you fear (FEAR – False Evidence Appearing Real). Remember – where you are now is not where you're going to be forever; this is all just for today.

- I personally found the guiding principles that I was given in my Reiki training helpful. You might want to consider them as guidance for each day you live through your divorce:

Just for today I will let go of anger.

Just for today I will let go of worry.

Just for today I give thanks for my many blessings.

Just for today I will do my work honestly.

Just for today I will be kind to every living thing (including myself).

PREVENTS

Bad communication, feeling stupid or judged, unworthy or ashamed – we can feel all these emotions in our bodies as we go through a divorce. If your divorce is a sh*tstorm, it's going to be impacting your body as well as your mind, and an increased amount of cortisol is never helpful (it reduces the happier hormone dopamine, as I described in the Introduction). Not only is this stress exhausting for your body, but it increases the likelihood of:

- Headaches
- Muscle tension or pain
- Chest pain
- Divorce brain fog
- Upset stomach/bowel problems
- Sleep problems

- Weight loss/gain
- Lower immunity
- Hair loss

Your body is your best barometer as to how you're feeling at any given time. If you haven't eaten, you get 'hangry'; if you don't drink enough water, you get a headache; if you feel anxious, your belly may be in knots. Make checking in with your body a routine part of preparing for those difficult times so you're better able to prevent conflict. What can you do to help yourself to feel even a tiny bit more relaxed about the difficulty you're facing?

Be focused, committed and kind during times of stress and conflict to help prevent your body from taking the hit – your body needs you and you need it!

Self-care is your superpower.

POOR

Divorce can get very expensive if you're not on it, prepared and ready for meetings. You may encounter challenges like moving house, finding a new job or racking up big bills – all while you're arguing with each other through your lawyers. Take responsibility for getting your household accounts in order, get your paperwork in order and read the documents you need to understand to maximise your knowledge and get good value from the time you're paying for with those professionals.

Conflict is expensive:
you either pay to get into it or you end up
paying to get out of it.

Manage your wellbeing so you're in the best place you can be, which may prevent you from making poor (and costly) decisions and saying or doing things you later regret – or that come out in front of your kids and those you love. This is the less expensive and less conflictual route through your divorce. When the DMMs jump in with their thoughts of survival, worries about an unfair division of finances and fears of the future, you need to be in the best shape to navigate the unexpected curve balls that present themselves.

If you're feeling overwhelmed, ask for help from a friend, sibling, parent or professional to give yourself the best opportunity to get through your divorce with a bigger financial pot at the end.

PERFORMANCE

"We all have to do what we don't want to do to get to where we want to go" is something that I said to myself when my DMMs were messing with my head, pushing me into the conflict shadow areas and taking me away from my Intention of a kinder divorce. But you get to choose to step into a new way of being; you get to choose who you want to be and how to do this divorce thing differently – hopefully better and kinder.

Why can't you and your Ex both be brilliant by choosing to thank each other for showing up, acknowledging the courage you both need to be sitting together in your rawest emotional state and talking about all the things that matter most – like children and money? Whether your Ex appears to be on board or not, you don't know how they're truly feeling inside. Honouring your commitment to doing what needs to be done as well as you can is a game-changer, whether it is after mediation, a lawyer's meeting, a family event or a pick-up/drop-off.

A word in here about boundaries, which are important. You don't have to become, think, like or see yourself as a doormat who lets others walk all over them; instead, stay with being a bigger person for your future mental and emotional health. Kindness is clever, no matter what your Ex chooses to say or do.

Give yourself permission to trust in the power of hope. Trust in yourselves that you can do this, with the help of your support squad and each other. You're both project-managing your way out of your marriage without a blueprint, maybe using the parts that once worked for you both to create a basic framework; therefore, don't allow your egos and the DMMs to stand in your way.

Remember: you matter, and your actions, words and thoughts can make a difference. Keep going, and never stop preparing.

Finance Fears

We are forever hopeful about money, finances and abundance – that we'll get the divorce settlement we want, that we'll find the perfect future home, that school fees/after school clubs will continue, or that we'll find ourselves a future partner who will end our worries around money (those niggly worries that link arms so easily through divorce). On those days when you feel the monetary madness is getting to you, take yourself off to your future, see beyond what's happening now, and trust that you'll be okay. Never lose hope in a happy and secure future for you and your family, no matter what your divorce throws at you.

This section doesn't sort your finances out or direct you to that magical gold pot under the right rainbow – yet it does talk about changing your mindset around finances, which is where hope comes in. If you're approaching your divorce finances with the DMMs firmly in place, this can lead to a whole lot of trouble – expensive trouble at that. It's not rocket science, so why do we have to make it so complicated? If you communicate honestly and openly, you can choose to get yourselves out of the divorce mess with more in that pot for each of your futures. Stay with hope!

Ask yourself this: why does it make sense for you to pay to argue and fight?

Divorce finance fears are generally attached to phrases like "fight for what's mine", "how dare they" and "it's the principle". Everyone going into divorce has finance on their minds – it's a favourite subject too for the DMMs – and whether there is fairness or perceived fairness is a place for conflict, which is why it's so important that you have good, trusted support and advice from your lawyer, mediator, financial planner and coach. With good advice and a fair-minded approach, you can work out a respectful plan that you can both accept – including the acknowledgement that neither of you will be 100% happy with the settlement!

I had an Instagram message from a lovely divorcee telling me she is trying to be honest and fair. Her Ex earns the most money and she is more vulnerable financially. She said he'd recently taken out a loan and signed a lease, so now he's not so great on paper and is less able to pay standard child maintenance. Her two questions were – how is this okay, and why does he get the power where money is concerned?

As I don't know the backstory, I'm going to speak generally about the unkindness that pervades divorces – but I'd refer this one straight to the karma bank! What bit about being a parent makes it okay to do this to your Ex? If punishing your Ex is part of your plan, you also punish your children, which is neither kind nor acceptable in today's society. But it happens a lot, and if you're in the camp where you think it's okay to punish your Ex financially and provide less for your children, you may want to ask yourself what unresolved emotions you're holding on to – and perhaps think about getting a therapist or coach.

The second question relates to power. If your Ex chooses to punish you, it is you who has the power ultimately over your thoughts and feelings, words and actions around money. Remember the two arrows? Spending time hating your Ex because they're being a total arse around money is haemorrhaging your lovely energy, which is best focused on you – whether it's creating a business that is going to support you, getting that dream job or some other strategy. Refocus, think hopeful thoughts, and make your money situation about you and not your Ex.

My golden rule on finance and divorce is this: where you are now is not your final destination, and the best is yet to come.

Imprint these words into your mind, heart, body and soul and believe them, rather than focusing on your end financial figure being your total. Trust that there will be opportunities to change your financial situation through work, retraining (if you want to) and consolidating your finances with a future partner. Divorce isn't the end of your life, it really is just the beginning of another.

I am big on trusting the universe to be there to support us, and I subscribe to the Law of Attraction (a philosophy that suggests positive thoughts bring positive results into a person's life), so do the personal work each day, stick with positive future thoughts, trust in the karma bank, keep cool, never lose hope – and stay kind.

Here are my thoughts and strategies for getting your money DMMs straight – before the financials get too messy.

Kindness

Kindness is a helpful and wise behaviour when it comes to money, and kind behaviour may lead to kinder divorce outcomes. It also:

- Helps you resist being triggered, and stops you from punishing yourself if you are.
- Helps you hold yourself accountable – basically, so you don't behave like an assh*le!

- Helps you start responding rather than reacting – by supporting you to keep your cool rather than indulge your fury.

Don't underestimate how kindness can help you save money through divorce. It can make all the difference. It doesn't mean that the other person has to play ball in the kindness park with you, but it saves you anxiety from those reactive rather than responsive decisions that might otherwise cost you.

Have you ever met a rich divorcee who got everything they wanted in their settlement, and whose anger was still burning inside them? You can feel it, right? All those unresolved emotions sit inside them, waiting to burst out when they least expect it – which could be lining up to damage a future relationship.

Giving in to anger and revenge can leave you feeling their negative effects for years. Punishing your Ex for what they did or didn't do comes from a place of anger and disempowerment. When you apply kindness to the divorce process, you are empowering yourself with the belief that you will be okay, rather than fuelling yourself with grudges from the past.

Words

Being aware of your words every time you communicate with your Ex (either in writing, in person, on the phone or via text) can save you money. Get good at sitting on what you've written or you're about to say. Go and make yourself a cup of tea before you press send, or show a friend who is grounded in common sense (rather than that friend who hates your Ex – perhaps with good reason). Get them to read through your communications and remove, reduce and relieve the inflammatory trigger words that can ramp up anger, frustration and resentment – and ultimately lead to extra costs for retaliatory letters from your Ex's lawyers.

Actions

Every time you see your Ex – whether you're dropping off children, picking them up, having a meeting or going into mediation – be responsible for your actions. Check in with 'that look' you know is on your face, or the rolling of the eyes, or the crossing of the arms – in other words, the defensive body language that may have triggered your Ex throughout your marriage, especially towards the end. Change it up – if it hasn't worked before, is it going to be helpful or work for you now? There's nothing more a scorned Ex loves than to be able to dig their heels in still further.

Remember: increased conflict = decreased money!

Thoughts

Where your thoughts go your energy goes, and if you are always thinking about your Ex and what they have and what you don't, this is not self-kindness on any level. You are hurting yourself if all you're choosing to look at is how your Ex has more money, a bigger house, a wealthy partner, lots of holidays away, expensive presents for the kids, and so on. You're in your Ex's backyard way too much – in effect, you're giving them all your lovely energy rather than sorting yourself out. Notice when you're doing this and take that all-important self-kindness step back into your own backyard; nourish yourself, tend to what you can bring to the table and start appreciating what you have.

This is what Ali had to say about divorce and money: "The hardest thing for me to do was hold my sh*t together when faced with my Ex turning up in his new (looks at me, trying not to laugh) mid-life crisis car. My much-loved and trashed kids' wagon, covered in drinks cartons, mud and football boots, with a big dent in the side as a result of divorce morning fog in the school carpark, made me feel angry. I felt I was left to pick up the pieces, and I knew I'd financially struggle to replace Gloria (the kids' car). It used to eat me up. I'd go to such a dark place about money until I realised I had to let that stuff go. Slowly, I realised that it was making me ill and that I had to channel my anger into finding ways to grow my money for me and appreciate that I had Gloria!"

Try this: I recommend you check out my powerful, effective How to Stop Thinking About Your Ex Course, which teaches you to get out of your Ex's backyard! (Go to the Divorce Goddess link in the Resources section.)

Sleep

Getting financially savvy is also about self-care. Dragging your sleep-deprived body around each day is doing you no good. I know sleep is hard to come by and difficult when you're stressed and going through separation or divorce, but do try to get to bed early.

If you are sleep-deprived, are you someone who is more likely to be grumpy, to react rather than respond, and to make mistakes? This is where the extra financial costs of divorce and living as a single parent can ramp up. You have a kindness over conflict choice here, so try to gift yourself more sleep (or at least time to read in bed to get yourself settled).

Emotions

Being more present before you go into any financial negotiation takes you out of your head and gives you an opportunity to ignore the fear-mongering DMMs, with their hellfire and brimstone thoughts. Growing your awareness around your emotions and your divorce finances is the key to better financial success in your divorce – you are empowered when you have this self-awareness and can keep the anger and angst at bay. Perhaps check in with whether you are caught up in the 'fight, flight or freeze' modes (refer to the Introduction) and if you are still struggling, make the necessary adjustments as per the 5Ps (earlier in this chapter) to increase your self-kindness and self-care and release your emotional stress.

Confession: I'd always struggle to get grounded around the Full and New Moon (every two weeks), and I'd likely be grumpy, be more triggered and say stuff that I'd regret – and then I'd beat myself up for not getting it right. If you have a big financial meeting or you're in mediation during emotional or hormonal times for you, try to exercise more self-care through awareness.

Business mode

Get out of your emotions and into the mindset that your divorce is a business deal – perhaps the biggest personal deal you will do in your life. Would you sit opposite a potential business partner as you would expect to do in a divorce? Do you go in bristling, defensive, angry, resentful and scared? No. You leave your ego at the door and pull out all the charm stops so you get the best deal – the financial and emotional kind, and it doesn't come with p*ssing someone off.

Get good at dropping into 'business' mode by taking the emotional parts out of key decisions – remember, your divorce deal is about focusing on the children first (if you have them), and then you.

The Magic 24

Whether you've received some bad news or just had a stressful day, allow yourself to feel it so you are best able to process your experiences. Give yourself 24 hours to sit on it so you can respond rather than react – when you do, you can take a breath and make that wiser, calmer and kinder decision. If you dive straight in without thinking, planning or adjusting to difficult news or experiences, this may make an expensive difference.

Once you do this a couple of times, you start to build that all-important neural pathway of taking the time out before you respond, which will make this helpful behaviour easier to drop into in the future as you go through the divorce process.

Preparation

Get yourself organised for meetings so that not a penny or minute is wasted and the inevitable fees don't cost you the earth. Ask for help from a friend; read up on what you need to for each meeting; and reread each email/letter from your lawyer/mediator and your Ex. If it feels relentless and you just want someone to take over, I get it, especially if you've never done anything like this before –

which is why you need to look after yourself and give yourself time to prepare. It is also great training for your future as you empower yourself to take more responsibility and grow your confidence.

Try this: Divorce fog for many is a thing, so adopt good practices such as those below to help keep you up to date and feeling more empowered:

- Get yourself a divorce finance-specific file AND subject divider.
- After each meeting, type up your notes (and read them through before the next meeting).
- Set time aside each week to check in and review what needs to be done – and do it!
- Open emails and important letters, DO NOT avoid them – if you avoid them, it will be to your cost.

Preparation can make all the difference throughout your divorce – this is why it's an integral part of the 5Ps (from earlier in this chapter).

Your Ex

You are both in it together until you are both out of it, and if you have children you may be in each other's lives for years. Working together and seeing your divorce (especially the finance bit) without emotion is best done through 'project management' eyes. Although at times it may be difficult, frustrating and very hard (biting your tongue may be needed!), it is the best way to save you money through your divorce.

Try this: To keep your divorce on track, work well together by:

- Setting an agenda for the groundwork meetings between you and your Ex and sticking to it.
- Setting an alarm if you need to take it in turns to speak so you both get three minutes.
- Listening properly and not interrupting (if you know you're going to upset each other – damage limitation, maybe).
- Using the parts of your personalities that work well together and complement each other rather than the parts that are conflicting. If one person is more methodical and the other an ideas person, work with your fantastic talents, rather than you both sitting there thinking about the frustrating times when your Ex was either a control freak or an airhead.
- Thanking each other for doing this work.

Home Is Where the Heart Is

Breakups can send the DMMs into freefall. Under threat, there is nothing like selling the family home or splitting up worldly chattels to get us into the aforementioned fight, flight or freeze mode. It is now more than ever that we need to have a place to rest our exhausted and weary heads so we can feel safe, strong and more grounded. Nothing makes people more jittery than not knowing where they're going to be living or having to sell the family home. With eight house moves in nine years, with kids and dogs and managed mostly on my own, I now know what helps and what doesn't – and what I do know is this:

Home is in your heart, not in the bricks and mortar.

Moving house is one of the most stressful times in our lives – it's probably tucked under divorce on the 'life's most difficult' list. If divorce is the life lesson that helps you let stuff go, why do so many divorcees spend money, energy and time fighting to hold on to a family home? It's a place you hold dear, and maybe you see it as your future safe place right now – but try to see the house move as an opportunity to let go and get out of these 'holding on to' or 'grasping' operating modes. This is your chance to move on fully and find out what you do want, with the understanding that, as with any home, your next home may not be the home you grow old in.

Sarah lamented: "I didn't ask for this, to end up in an albeit lovely apartment. I wanted my old home, with everything we had built together inside it. I never saw myself living where I am now, it was so hard making the adjustment." We worked on aspects of gratitude – she was living nearer to her grandchildren, and in a more vibrant and welcoming community. We worked with the concept of acceptance to allay her anger over her much-reduced accommodation, settling the DMMs that sent her to dark places that left her feeling like a victim and with bodily emotions that were unhelpful to her health.

Sorting through your possessions

It's not just houses… humans are quite good at holding onto stuff. We build our homes, fill them with memories and collectables, and then the recalibration moment that is divorce arrives and we realise that it really is time to let go.

The division of our worldly chattels can unearth deeply held bitterness – with family heirlooms disappearing to the 'other' side, the loss of favourite vinyl collections and the splitting of so many memories. The sense of attachment can sneak up and rob the kindness out of sensitively selling homes and dividing chattels.

A divorce that is underpinned with kindness rather than conflict will still be asking you to make tough choices – choices based on whether you choose to open up your tea chest of fears or not. How ready are you to let your fears go and work with your Ex to find a workable solution?

A client, David, said, "We both had to work hard at this, remembering that when we worked well together in the past, we really were an indomitable force of mutual support. Going through our attic was utterly soul-destroying, something we had both dreaded, and yet it was incredibly cathartic. We got to acknowledge the good stuff about our lives together (with many tears), we integrated the compatible skills we'd used in previous shared projects, and this was such an unexpected gift in all the emotional fallout. It gave us an unexpected foundation on which to build a better relationship moving forwards."

Try this: With a kindness hug, I offer these suggestions for sorting through your shared possessions during these painful, tough and sad times:

- Start clearing from the top of your home and work down.
- Make a list of the rooms and what is in each, then go through each list, ticking:
    - What you want and what you don't want

- What you can sell (to pay legal bills, moving costs, and so on)
- What you can gift with love to someone who will feel the love too (I love Marie Kondo's idea of thanking things and letting them go with love to someone else).

- Resolve potential conflict over possessions by taking a kind approach:
  - Scale 1–10 on the pieces you both want and why (remember, communicate now rather than harbour resentment for years to come!).
  - Be generous with each other if you know one loves something more than you – remember, kindness rather than conflict.
  - If you are tempted by your Ex's family heirlooms, just give them back to them. Ask yourself, if you are in any doubt, how it would feel to have them in your home knowing they had belonged to your Ex's grandmother (for example). Do you want to fill your home with love and happiness or objects attached to resentment?

The deconstruction of your home can be a hellish process, but you can choose to dismantle it gently, organise yourselves and let stuff go. Send the attachment DMMs to the farthest corner of the world on your sorting days so you can get into the right headspace for letting go of once-valued possessions and leaving emotional attachments in the past.

Helen said that she and her husband came to a sticking point with some glass lamp bases that she had always loved very much. He suddenly decided he wanted them. He wouldn't budge; she knew he was goading her, and she realised that although she loved them, there would be others out there she could buy. She said that it felt so ridiculous but it was important to her to keep them, until she had this flash of clarity around attachment and told him he could have them. She saw in his eyes the disappointment that she didn't care, and she knew she had won because she had let go of the need to have them. Three days later, he left a message saying he had reconsidered as he knew she loved them, so she could have them!

Letting go of the family home

Saying goodbye to your family home, whether it was palatial, a semi or a flat, still brings the same emotions – it was your shared home, with memories of first nights, unpacking, children and family gatherings. The fabric of your life as a family and as a couple is waiting to be divided on the divorce table – and sadly, it presents you with a perfect battlefield opportunity on which to wage war (should you decide to do so).

Kimberley shared this story with me: "I remember as a child, my father shouting late one Sunday night, 'Your mother has had an affair', with my mother screaming, 'No, don't tell them like this' and then hearing 'And this house is going too'. I ran away. I sat behind a wall in the village in the pouring rain at the age of 11, asking myself over and over again what was going to happen to us, our pets and where were we going to live? It was foremost in my mind, because it was so sudden and said in anger. It was pivotal to me, not feeling safe in my childhood anymore, and that continued well into my adulthood."

Whether you end up with the family home or it is sold, see it as an opportunity to rebuild. Get curious about the adventure of settling in and creating a new home for your new life. Try not to be afraid of what the DMMs are telling you. I remember feeling so relieved that our big family home had gone – I just wanted something manageable, cosy and safe that contained everything I truly loved rather than everything I thought I wanted.

If you're finding yourself holding on to your family home for reasons other than pure love, ask yourself why. Is it the shame of a downsize? Is it to mess with your Ex? Or is it because you can use it as part of your 'for the children' arsenal of conflict?

If the DMMs are making their presence known with unhelpful thoughts around moving to a smaller house, ask yourself:

- Does it really matter where you live, as long as you are safe, warm and your home is filled with love?
- Why would you want to hold on to something that can only serve as a reminder of what you had, rather than move out and wish it well for someone else?
- If you are okay and happy in a new home, won't the children be okay and happy with this too?
- Do you want to prolong or increase conflict?

If holding on is based on the fear of the unknown, remind yourself just how *unknown* your life has been recently. Accept and embrace the fact that you do already have the life skills you need to grow your confidence, embody the change and go for it, all the way!

A note about pets

Divorce doesn't just impact shared homes, possessions and finances (plus of course arrangements around childcare where needed). We need to talk about the house elves, house dragons or simply – if you are more inclined to the normal – our family pets.

To keep or not keep the family pets is another source of potential conflict. Maybe one of you never particularly cared for the family's pets, which makes for an easy outcome.

Sadly, however, family pets are increasingly becoming a source of conflict in divorce. They're being added to the list of chattels in the same way as a car or any other possession, with pet ownership either being transferred to one party or the other, or leading to wrangling over an agreement to share custody. (Pet maintenance costs should also be taken into consideration regarding your finances, including kennel and pet-sitting costs, vet's bills and insurance, and food.)

Our pets sit deep in our hearts. When couples split, pets can be a real source of comfort while you get used to the idea of living alone. Maybe take a minute to think about how your Ex feels. Could you both agree to share the pets (at least for now), which might be an easier and kinder way forward?

Try this: If pets are a part of your household, consider adding kind outcomes relating to your pets to your Divorce Intention.

Hope for the future

Hold hope for your future home in your heart as you navigate your way into it courageously and kindly, keeping in mind the following:

- It doesn't matter where you live, it is about creating a heart-filled, safe home.

- Even in your most stressed moments, you still have your very valuable gut instinct, intuition and your inner voice telling you whether a certain property is right for you or not – please try to trust yourself and listen!

- People are good, kind and they want to help, so ask for help!

- Being humble about your changing life situation is what truly brings out the empathetic part of people, and they will pull out all the stops to help you (I was once offered a toffee to help me stop crying in the estate agents – and I got a hug, too).

- Embrace the opportunity to experiment with your new (or old) home and create a home that truly fills you with warmth, happiness and safety every time you walk in the door.

- Try to share the furniture with your Ex so there is familiarity in each home for the children.

- Fairy lights have a big part to play in making somewhere feel magic – indulge me, please!

- Marie Kondo's book *The Life-Changing Magic of Tidying* is a must if you are downsizing – she offers advice on letting go of possessions and even gifting them to others who may find more joy in them, another act of kindness all round.
- Shopping in charity shops, online and at furniture emporiums is so much fun!
- You can help your Ex put their home together (and if you want, let them help you too) to show support for each other through this very stressful process.
- Building flat-packed furniture is indeed an accomplishment, and so is buying your very own toolkit and using it!

It is easy to feel lost at the end of a relationship, lacking trust in your own judgement or abilities. Remaking your new home is the most wonderful opportunity of self-discovery and another foundational stone for you to reconnect to who you really are and remember what you really love. This is your opportunity to reset your life, and if it means beginning again then so be it. Have some fun – divorce doesn't have to be fraught and exhaustingly competitive; instead, it can be an opportunity to create and nurture hope for the future through kindness.

Remember, kindness can be clever too!

Although we humans are adverse to change, we are actually far more resilient than we give ourselves credit for. Hope is about choosing to see beyond the difficulties, pain and challenges that present themselves to us: to believe in life being something other than hardship and the daily grind. When you give your time and energy to hope, it grows – and hope becomes easier to drop into (rather than staying in the victim hole).

Remember:

H – Hope

O – Opportunities

P – People

E – Empowered

Part 2

A Kinder Journey

There's a moment just before we step into anything that feels scary or unknown – do or (hypothetically) die. It's that split second in which the divorce mind monkeys (DMMs) sense their opportunity to go all in, and they do! It's time to be your mind's best friend so you can work with it rather than against it. Finding yourself on the precipice of anything without a map or blueprint is when you put the ultimate trust in yourself and a kinder divorce process. Sometimes we have to trust that taking steps into the unknown with a good, authentic and honest heart is when we will be rewarded with life's sweet stuff.

In fight, flight or freeze mode, we can revert to listening to the DMMs rather than taking a step back, getting off the fast-flowing divorce walkway and getting out of our own way (by not trying to control everything). It's an ask, right? But then doesn't everything in life have something unknown at the end of it?

This Part is about discovering that peace already exists within you. The kinder journey involves reconnecting with yourself – your thoughts, words and actions. In this Part, you create an action plan to manage those tough days and reduce conflict by keeping a sense of balance and remembering that you are more powerful in all of this than you may currently believe.

Chapter 3

Accessing Peace

You may be laughing (but quietly dying) at the thought that peace could actually be a part of your life as you go through divorce. Peace and divorce are generally seen as being polar opposites. I would really love to guru the hell out of this chapter by saying I accessed peace but, honestly, having tried many times to find peace, I gave up, and in doing so allowed peace to find me.

Peace is a place I believe you come to unexpectedly. You stumble upon it when you look after yourself, you become understanding of others and you come to a place of acceptance. It can be on those early mornings before the house wakes up when you have your first cup of tea or coffee; it might be a rainbow appearing unexpectedly in the sky that stops you in your tracks with a wow moment; or after a good, productive meeting with your Ex. You can access it just before the DMMs remind you that fight, flight or freeze mode is safer. As many of us go through life on automatic pilot (see the Introduction), especially during stressful events such as divorce, we often don't see the cunning of our DMMs telling us we'll never attain the dizzy heights of peace; we may be too tired to challenge them and thus we fall out of our 'peace' without realising we were there in the first place, if only for a moment.

Maybe then we can work with making your mind your friend. Think of a puppy going out on a lead for the first time. It is curious, wants to explore everywhere and doesn't yet know how to walk beside you. Think of your mind as the puppy – when we spend time guiding it to walk beside us and speaking kindly to it, rather than fighting and being unkind to it, the puppy learns quicker and everything becomes easier. Mindfulness and meditation was what turned my divorce mental and emotional wellbeing around so my mind became my friend, not my conflictual enemy. These practices were my mind's (puppy's) training so I could work with the DMMs rather than have them running my life and being unhelpful.

To start with, we have to learn how to get out of our own way and to stop making life harder for ourselves. Each of us are in our own little boat on the big river of life. Instead of trusting the downstream flow of the river, we spend our lives rowing upstream trying to control life, especially when we feel threatened by the unknown. When almost everything in your life has just imploded, the need to hang on to every branch, bit of wood or boat travelling down the river out of fear is REAL. With the go-to narrative that divorce can only be bad, it's no surprise that peace eludes us; we try to control everything, stuck in fight, flight and freeze modes, and we continue to think the future destination will be worse. We get exhausted, scared and miss so much of what is good, which robs us of our peace because we feel we have to control things, often out of fear. It can be so difficult to trust in the flow of life and see where it takes us, especially through divorce, so we try to take control. In trying to take control, we can get ourselves in the way of what is supposed to happen, with our thoughts, words and actions (such as trying to make your Ex speak or do something in the way you think they should, which becomes their opportunity to treat you to more digging in of heels, which may increase their resistance to being kind). This is when unnecessary conflict occurs within ourselves, which we can prevent by making peace with ourselves first and working with acceptance that we can't control what our Ex says, does or thinks, which may otherwise ripple out into our world as greater conflict. This may all sound a little airy-fairy to some of you, and I get it, but think back to when you let go of the outcome you most wanted but had no control over (such as the sale of the family home falling through and delaying the divorce process, and then suddenly out of the blue a month later you have two bidders that come in at a higher price so you end up with more money!). There are always reasons why things don't happen as we want them to – the trick is to take that step back, be the observer (rather than 'getting your knickers in a twist') and remember to check in with gratitude for the original outcome that didn't occur (for more on gratitude, see 'The Power of Gratitude' in Chapter 4). Sometimes we aren't able to see what is best for us at the time; anyway, I challenge you to find an example from your own experiences!

If you are someone who wrestles with control, peace is going to be tougher to access. Try to see your divorce as a process that helps you access peace by teaching it to you, admittedly the hard way, and maybe many times over. Is it time to stop trying to control what is happening, practise letting go, even a little, and start getting out of your own way, seeing this as a gift?

Ask yourself this: is it not time for you to come from a place of courage and trust so you take responsibility and respond, rather than reacting and handing your power away – using up all that energy with the conflict associated with grabbing and hanging on because you can't trust that you'll be okay to float down the river to somewhere better?

In this chapter, I'll share with you why the eternal, elusive power of peace is actually within you already. We'll look at:

- Self-discovery through divorce – who are you?
- How you really can find peace on the difficult days and change your mindset so you thrive rather than survive

- Managing conflict – what works and what doesn't
- The magical powers of forgiveness and forgetting
- How to make loneliness your friend
- Why spinning many plates is a terrible idea for life balance
- The delights of self-care and why it is so very important

Self-Discovery

How much peace do you want in your life – what are you ready to settle for? Again, we are back to choice. You can continue doing what you've always done and get what you think you deserve, or you can try self-discovery with yourself every day to inch yourself closer to peace within yourself. It begins with kindness to yourself and really, if you cannot love yourself, how are you going to be able to love somebody else (food for future thought!). So granted, there may not be much love in the mix for your Ex, but self-love or self-kindness, whichever is easier for you, begins with acknowledging, empowering and trusting YOU. (Chapter 1 is all about self-kindness, so head back there if you need a refresher.)

Try this: Give yourself 24 hours to see how many times you do yourself down or are hard on yourself. Ask yourself, "Do I need any more negativity in my life?" For example, "I'm so stupid" or "My life is a mess" plus all those 'shoulds' ("I should be coping better") – you get my drift? Be gentle with yourself and try to change the words to "I'm learning to…" or "I can do this…"

Sit for 10 minutes somewhere quiet where you won't be disturbed. Close your eyes, have your hands on your lap and take a couple of deep breaths into your belly.

Bring to mind a time when life was fun and you were doing things you loved to do (rather than because your Ex wanted to do them). Allow yourself this self-time to settle into how you feel as you think back. Sometimes this can be difficult because we are biased towards the negative. If this is the case, take a breath and go a little bit deeper. Think of belly laughing with a friend, your first holiday away, the first time you walked out of the front door as a teenager and owned it, being a 20-something going out to your first job, becoming completely absorbed in a hobby you used to love… find the time when you were confident, outlandishly bold and happy (if not all, then certainly one of these!).

Feel into that feeling, immerse yourself into the energy of that time, that moment, and notice what comes up for you. Are the DMMs jumping in with thoughts to distract you? Go back in and enjoy, be curious as to what it was that made you feel this way. Notice how your body is feeling now – light and tingly, or heavy and relaxed?

What memories are coming up for you to remind you of who you were, and are still, even though you feel like your 'inner funny' has maybe disappeared? Write down what came up for you – did you love wearing a certain colour? Were you once good at something that you forgot about? Were you the funny person? Or a good friend? Connect to how you're feeling; bank it if you like, so it's there as a reminder that the old you is still alive inside. It may not feel like that at times, but the more you tune into the parts that make up the best of you, the more you grow them.

Self-discovery is all about finding or re-finding yourself, seeing what works now and what doesn't and making the changes. This might be booking a holiday just for you, taking up an old hobby again, or starting to go to comedy gigs with friends to kick-start your buried inner funny. It might be dying your hair a different colour, getting a tattoo, wearing different clothing – thanks divorce diet! I met a 55-year-old man who said he always wanted a bright red pair of shoes and now was the time to buy them. He said he didn't care that he was middle-aged, it was his life – love him for that!

Or Juliet, who bought her first bright red sexy underwear set aged 42. "I didn't care whether anyone saw it or not, I bought it for me and every time I wore it, I smiled because only I knew I had such great underwear on. I felt empowered and alive for the first time in many years – I was released from silly limitations and blocks about sexy underwear only worn by others – plus, I wore it to our mediation sessions just for the sheer self-confidence it brought me!"

Please do whatever works for you – try as much fun and new stuff as you can, so that you can find more smiles and lighten your day because life is way, way too short not to embark on a journey of self-rediscovery!

Finding Peace on Difficult Days

Writing this chapter really took me back to my divorce days. If anyone had suggested finding peace then, I would have grabbed it, no matter what it looked like, and hung on for dear life! I'm not able to give you the antidote to chaos, pain and raw emotions, but I want to share with you how I discovered peace and was able to revisit it again and again.

So, if you aren't living in a monastery on the side of a mountain in the Himalayas and sitting for hours meditating, mindfully living every moment and having the ability to let go of whatever negatively affects you, then here are a bunch of different tools to help you with finding peace. These tools found me, a) showing up when I needed them and b) kind of kicking me in the head to listen.

I remember one day being literally in my head; I had so many thoughts around survival, conflict and guilt that I was actually light-headed, wasn't paying attention, walked into a cupboard door and really hurt my head. It was like the Universe had opened that door to make me listen and was saying, "Tosh, just STOP overthinking and pay more attention!" I found myself smiling – maybe from slight concussion or blinding realisation, it was like I was being forced to slow down.

Notice what signs appear to encourage you to be more present (obviously ones that don't hurt so much!). What makes you take your foot off the accelerator and slows you down, literally?

If your head is full of anxious thoughts and worries about the future, it's probably time to start making a change. Realistically, you're only ever going to SURVIVE if you're living in your head, because, in all honesty, it is f*cking exhausting. As the ever-insightful scientist Bruce Lipton says: "To fully thrive, we must not only eliminate the stressors but also actively seek joyful, loving, fulfilling lives that stimulate growth processes." AMEN! You can't THRIVE without understanding that to do so, you need to change your habits, lifestyle and commit to yourself.

And the irony of life is this: it is only when you walk into the clamouring thoughts in your head that you get the opportunity to find peace. If you spend time trying to escape what's happening in the moment (understandable), ask yourself – are you 'doing' rather than 'being'? We begin as young children wishing that we were in the year above at school, then when we're older that we could escape the reins of parental supervision. We can spend our lives perpetually wishing to be somewhere else: "When I move out it will all be okay" or "When I get my divorce papers through, it will all be over..." erm... nope! The work of self-care, self-discovery and self-kindness is ongoing; the sooner you begin, the less pain you'll feel.

Take two couples I worked with, both couples divorcing due to an affair. The difference between them was this: one of the women wanted to properly punish her husband for cheating on her, and the other chose not to. Consider the similarities and differences between their experiences.

Katrine was a "good trophy wife" in her words through gritted teeth, feeling like a "fecking Irish fool" being a competitive perfectionist wife. She remembered the 1950s 'Good Wife Guide' that her ex-hippie mum had sent her one day for a laugh, with a note encouraging her to do things a little differently – to keep growing and learning (something Katrine pushed against). Katrine hated herself for not retraining and getting a job, but she hated her "bastard" husband David more. Katrine started working with me after she felt exhausted at trying to punish everyone, and especially herself. She said she craved peace from the angry place inside but that it would forever elude her. We worked with simple practices like guided meditations that focused on her body and breathing rather than her difficult thoughts, and she started to reclaim her inner peace through this focus and by being kind to herself.

You can find a link to some helpful meditations in the Resources section.

Jessica, a stay-at-home mum, was crushed, ashamed and deflated after the shock of Jack's affair. Jessica's confidence was low; failure and betrayal featured heavily in her thoughts, but in quieter moments out walking the dog she realised that their marriage had been in trouble for the last five years. Neither she nor Jack communicated about their problems; she'd mentioned couples counselling and Jack had angrily brushed it aside. Jessica didn't want to fight Jack through their divorce; she thought Jack would fight, but she still wanted to try the kinder route. We worked on her Divorce Intention, and I introduced her to a lawyer, mediator and financial planner. Jessica shared her Intention with Jack. In her words, "Telling Jack I wanted a 'kind' divorce with our dignity, finances and ability to co-parent intact was the most empowering thing I've said in years." Jessica said at that moment she found a sense of inner peace. She noticed how her body relaxed, a heavy weight lifted and she felt relief. Jack expected to be given a good divorce flailing, was relieved and, with a new-found respect for his wife, cried openly in the meeting saying that he wanted this too but was too scared to say so. Jessica continued to check herself each time she made a conscious decision to not fall into the victim blame pit and, yes, she felt peace. She banked these feelings, noted them in her journal and regularly reread them when she felt any anger rising that she wanted to direct at Jack. She didn't always hold her tongue – "I'm not a bloody angel" – but she said that being more mindful for most of the time, aided by her Intention, helped enormously.

Both these ladies found peace by making time away from their busy thoughts, training the DMMs to be less noisy and bossy and trying to act with kindness.

Throughout this book there are opportunities to practise self-care mentally and emotionally, spiritually and physically. You are in control of finding your own peace; sadly, it doesn't just appear when the Decree Absolute is in your hand. So, you have a choice: start right now and nail the DMMs or stay in 'no peace limbo'. It's all about introducing the DMMs to kinder habits as early as you can.

Finding your peace in your divorce is up to you.

Try this: Having your own tool kit of 'go-to' practices that take the heat out of the DMMs, that you know work for you, is like giving yourself a hug:

- Practise this breathing technique: "I breathe in peace; I breathe out worries"
- Say thank you for 100 things (hard, but such a game-changer)
- Write a reminder list of what you can and can't control
- Take 24 hours away from social media
- Stand on the grass in your bare feet – yep, really! – it's good for helping you feel more grounded
- Try not complaining AT ALL for a day
- Use the Ho'oponopono practice (see the section 'Forgiveness is Healing' later in this chapter for more on this)
- Try cold sea swimming – so good for resetting emotions and letting go of mental noise
- Find a cosy armchair/bed to curl up in, read a book and drink tea
- Have a bath – in the middle of the day to be extra decadent – for some nurturing me-time

Try them all out; feel into what works and what doesn't work for you rather than copying what someone else does. Do 'you' first, always!

Managing Conflict

Even though conflict is almost inevitable in highly emotional divorces, this book is about the options you have on how to best manage it and have the most peaceful divorce you are capable of.

There's so much strength to be taken from your divorce by 'flipping' your thoughts, actions and words into something more positive. The more you do this, the more you feel empowered – brain training in action! There are opportunities for better-than-expected outcomes, more lightbulb moments and synchronistic life changes that benefit not just you but everyone.

Conflict is part of being human. It doesn't come from the part of us that loves a peaceful, loving and kind life without arguments and disagreements, but from the place that gives us the confidence to be heard and seen, and to stand up for what we feel is right. It's how you *manage* conflict that is the magical key in all of this. You can either smash through the door of conflict, battling and fighting, exhausting yourself, or go through it more kindly and gently using your key.

Try this: If your life is currently full of conflict, ask yourself these questions:

- Am I happy with a divorce life like this?
- In which areas of my divorce am I experiencing conflict?
- What can I do to minimise divorce conflict?

I'm inviting you to go from the battle zone to living with less conflict, and trusting that you can do so.

Juliet was furious when her Ex, George, said he couldn't pay her the full amount of maintenance for the month. She had savings to cover the shortfall, but she said she thought he had probably overspent on his carbon bike addiction (bloody MAMILs, or middle-aged men in Lycra) to punish her, be an "arse" and cause conflict. She had no idea that George had been made redundant and dreaded telling Juliet for fear of more shame, potential lack of future maintenance payments (until he got another job) and his biggest dread – Juliet stopping him seeing the children as "punishment". Juliet asked her lawyer to send a letter demanding why (costing her more money, which stressed her out). At the weekend pick-up/drop-off for the children, George confessed his redundancy to her. Juliet realised she'd jumped straight into conflict (her go-to), without considering there might be other reasons why George couldn't pay. It was a lesson to be more mindful of her rampaging DMMs and drop into a kinder operating mode.

Conflict happens more easily when we're caught up in our thoughts and on automatic pilot; that's when the DMMs have more power. They prevent us from seeing the fuller and bigger picture, so we react rather than respond. Checking in with ourselves and having a quiet word with our DMMs is taking ourselves off automatic pilot. This can be done by practising STOP (Stop, Take a breath, Observe and Proceed, explained fully in Chapter 2), having a daily mindfulness meditation (see my free Taster Mindfulness & Meditation Course at the Divorce Goddess link in the Resources section) and being more present in life. In this way we increase our ability to be more aware so we can respond rather than react to potential conflict, giving it less fertile ground on which to grow.

One of the most useful tools for getting off automatic pilot is to focus fully on whatever you're doing in the moment. Be present with what you're doing and tune into the five senses (sight, smell, touch, taste and hearing) as you take a shower in the morning, drink a cup of tea or walk up the stairs. Keep bringing your thoughts back to the smell of the shower gel, the heat of the mug as you hold it or the movements of your legs as you climb the stairs. The more you are present, the greater the 'buffer zone' –

the split-second judgement space as to whether you enter into conflict or you choose a wiser, calmer way forward. You're training the *observing muscle* (or the *buffer space muscle* – the space between reactive and responsive thoughts) that you can then use to take the heat out of difficult and conflictual thoughts. It may be difficult to believe that integrating simple everyday practices into daily lives can help reduce conflict, but it does, it just takes – as ever – a little practice.

The key is in creating the habit of stepping out of your random and thus limiting thoughts into a space of conscious, powerful choice. Conflict can arise in a mediation meeting, a co-parenting event (think birthdays) or by sending a text after wine late at night. Getting good at stopping your DMMs in their tracks, reclaiming your grace and dignity by not 'losing it', is what you do have control over.

Our bodies are an incredible barometer of how we feel about conflict (such as feeling like you've been punched in the gut by a message from your Ex). It may be that your divorce-fogged head hurts as it's filled with unhelpful, unkind thoughts, or your breath becomes shallow and your shoulders begin to tighten up. Your body tells you when you're stressed, so notice and use these signs as a reminder to step back and get clarity, respond better and act more productively.

Self-kindness through conflict is something else you have control over. Self-loathing is conflict's friend, so firstly I suggest you stop everything you may be doing that you hate yourself for. If you're in conflict with yourself, you're likely to be in conflict with others.

Conflict with yourself may look like:

- A bottle of wine on your own on a school night, with next-day shame because you can't think straight, the children play up, plus you have the oh-so-attractive 'shot eye' look.

- Regret that you phoned your friend who hates your Ex rather than your calmer friend just before mediation or a collaborative session, which ramps up the DMMs so you lose it over something small. Time and session costs are wasted and your Ex is riled.

- Making it difficult for your Ex and their new partner to see and have fun with the children due to your weekend plans being cancelled because you're angry and resentful. This upsets the kids, and you feel like crap over your weekend off, compounding your feelings of guilt, failure and wretchedness.

- Saying something inflammatory to your Ex, which is going to set you both back in the process and cost more financially.

If this is you, firstly stop judging yourself, beating yourself up and feeling worse as a result. Secondly, commit to taking one kinder step towards NOT doing it again. Don't have wine in the house until the weekend, phone that friend who cares that important meetings work for you and your Ex, and notice when you're feeling vengeful and do something (like punching a pillow or going for a run) to mitigate how you're feeling.

Managing conflict in divorce is like trying to catch a box of escaping frogs blindfolded. It feels weird, you don't know quite what you're up against and generally you feel you've failed, until you have a lightbulb moment, where the blindfold drops off and you realise you can go through this process kindly and peacefully. Remember: you have control over adopting habits that support you to observe the triggers more easily and respond rather than react.

Dealing with a conflict-loving Ex

"My Ex loves conflict and drama" is something I hear often. Don't let your Ex steal your peace, dignity and grace, and do what you know is right. If this is truthfully the case (no drama from you ever, right?) – why not suggest, "Can we try to find ways to reduce conflict; do we need to pay to argue?" Or, write to your Ex and tell them you're not interested in fighting; reinforce how you feel and be committed – send or resend your Divorce Intention to remind them. Remember, your Ex doesn't have to agree, but you may be surprised what lands in their subconscious and makes the difference in the future when you least expect it. Be gentle with yourself; divorce life is hard. If you have a drama-loving partner, then let it become about you working for you, reducing conflict within yourself first. Let your Ex burn themselves out if they particularly want to hold all that anger and negative emotion for future relationship drama – you don't have to. Come back to focusing on your children if you have them, and give them the sanctuary of one parent who's not holding this conflict energy.

Growing your awareness of conflict

Managing conflict to access more peace is also being curious as to what is and what isn't conflict for you. Do certain situations leverage conflict? Or are things more likely to kick off at certain times in the month?

Grow your awareness!

A lot of clients I work with say their weeks can feel very conflictual! This exercise is to give you clarity on how much conflict there really is, as opposed to the DMMs telling you, in their dramatic fashion, "My life's so hard."

Try this: To get clarity when things feel tough, I invite you to think about:

- What is the current conflict and unpleasant event?
- How does it make me feel?
- Where do I feel it in my body?
- How can I change my thoughts around it?
- How can I do things differently?

Do this exercise when something unpleasant or conflictual happens, big or small, for a week, so you notice more how you act, think and what you say. Get used to making small adjustments (letting go of the small stuff), create a new neural pathway by doing this and develop a practice of self-kindness that includes time for you to be with challenging thoughts.

Try doodling, meditating on and then writing down your thoughts – getting them on paper gets them out of your head and gives you more breathing space.

Identifying where and why there's more conflict rather than it all being rolled into one gives you the opportunity to manage the DMMs telling you otherwise.

Here are some ways to reduce opportunities for the conflict DMMs to wade in (remember, awareness gives you choice!):

- Sleep on that inflammatory email. Ask yourself – what do I realistically want out of this? How will my actions affect the outcome if they're made when I'm stressed, angry or under pressure?

- Don't open the Friday solicitor's letter if it's not urgent – do you need this conflict to impact your weekend off or your precious time with your kids?

- Ask yourself – does being fighty, angry and drama-fuelled serve me? If you were known to be a little bit drama queened or kinged up in your marriage, try seeing your divorce as an opportunity to change this and surprise your Ex with just how cool you can really be.

Trust yourself: you can do this, and remember the mantra "You will not have my anger" – you are stronger than your Ex and your divorce mind monkeys.

Forgiveness is Healing

Forgiveness is a gift you can give yourself.

Forgiveness may seem like an unlikely coupling with divorce, but trust me – you want peace? You have to learn to forgive – this is where the ultimate healing happens.

WARNING! Nothing makes the mind monkeys rise up screaming with laughter or rage more than the suggestion that forgiveness is worth a punt through your divorce. "A shot in the dark, more like!" they'll shriek. If it's too painful to think about forgiveness at this stage, you're welcome to revisit this part when you feel ready. However, I urge you to read it so it lodges in your mind as a possibility as you move forwards.

Forgiveness is a powerful tool and is the healing; the not forgetting is the lesson.

The DMMs aren't great with you moving forwards and out of their control zone. The possibility of forgiveness in their eyes equates to making what your Ex did (or didn't do) to you okay. For the record, it doesn't, and this is the 'not forgetting' part of 'forgive and forget' turned on its head. The 'not forgetting' part is the lesson of how can you do things differently and how can you see this as something bigger than the painful experience. Your divorce is your opportunity, and forgiveness is the door to it!

If you're wondering why you need to spend time on this 'not forgetting and forgiveness', then try to see it as an exercise in healing for you, and you alone, moving forwards.

Everyone has been through stuff. Theirs may not be the same as yours, but know this: you are not alone. Stuff isn't just happening to you, it's also happening to millions of other people in the world.

How do you find a way to heal pain, heartbreak, mistakes and misgivings when you feel so raw and vulnerable? As ever, all this begins with YOU; you need to forgive yourself first. I mean, how can you start forgiving your Ex if you're angry with yourself for a) allowing this to have happened, b) getting a divorce, c) for not seeing it coming or d) not being honest with yourself in the first place?

I'm always amazed by how many people tell me they knew getting married to this person was wrong, but they either got caught up in the preparations, their partner or friends pressured them, or they thought this was their one and only chance. Interesting, right?

Robert said he hated himself for choosing to not see the signs that his marriage was in trouble. He said, "For a long time I couldn't forgive Sophia for her affair, I hated her with a vengeance. As Tosh and I started working with forgiveness, I realised that I needed to forgive myself before forgiving Sophia. I knew there were cracks in our marriage and I brushed the stuff I didn't want to look at under the carpet. I didn't have the confidence or courage to ask for help and I regret this deeply. I beat myself up

A LOT for not listening to my gut instinct and although I've started practising self-forgiveness, I'm still angry with myself and know it's going to take time. Divorce is full of hard lessons."

So, how do you begin to forgive yourself?

Try this: Forgiving yourself is about being with yourself, allowing yourself to lean into 'not getting it right' and it being okay and part of the process you are going through, so:

- Tuck up somewhere warm and cosy, like your bed.

- Have a big mug of tea and a box of tissues to hand, and turn off your mobile devices.

- Close your eyes if it feels good and start to take slow, deep breaths down into your belly. Breathe in for a count of four, and out for six. Imagine you are trying to inflate a balloon in there. (If you're not used to breathing like this, try not to expect too much of yourself; just do what is right for you.)

- Put your hands on your heart and allow your attention to come to the feel of the beat of your heart under your hands. Imagine you're breathing into and out of your heart. Notice when your DMMs want to take your attention elsewhere and bring yourself back to these breaths.

- Say to yourself, "I am okay, I am safe, I have my own back and I forgive myself." Take a few more breaths.

- Check in with how you feel after this – there's no right or wrong answer, it is just about observing your thoughts and experiences.

- 'See' your hands holding your heart safely and lovingly. Bring what you want to forgive yourself for to mind (it may take several attempts, which is okay; this work can be hard) and say the following, which comes from a wonderful Hawaiian forgiveness practice called Ho'oponopono:

  o I'm sorry for (whatever it is).

  o Please forgive me (forgive yourself, you did what you did with the tools you knew).

  o Thank you (for the opportunity and lesson to heal from what you're going through).

  o I love you (LOVE yourself for doing this work and accepting a dose of self-kindness).

Repeat however many times you need or want to, and often – after you've been too hard on yourself is always good!

Write anything down that you want to forgive. Bring this to mind; be aware of the intensity of the feelings and what is coming up for you when you focus on it. If your DMMs take you off into the story (to protect you), come back, take a breath and be with your feelings. Give yourself permission to be with what you're feeling. It is your experience; it is not right or wrong, it is simply what you did under the circumstances and you will be okay.

Robert used this tool many times over to work through the different layers and memories of painful times in his life that he found himself holding onto. Sometimes he would catch himself complaining about Sophia and would feel a gnaw in his heart. He would silently say the words of the Ho'oponopono practice to himself; it was a difficult concept for Robert, but he no longer wanted to carry the heaviness of what had happened. He found this practice allowed him to let go and he felt kinder towards himself.

Learning to forgive yourself first is such a powerful tool to heal your emotional wounds. By attending to yourself first, you heal yourself and grow the forgiveness muscle, which you may in time use to choose to forgive your Ex as well. When you begin to see the difference to your life by choosing not to beat yourself up and instead apply kindness, you start to move on, one day at a time.

This practice can also be used for your Ex, family members, work colleagues, or anyone who has caused you pain or peed you off!

This forgiveness stuff is hard; we know it is good to do, but it is still tough. As ever, you can choose not to do the whole forgiveness thing and stay angry about everything your Ex did or is doing to you. But this means you're still letting what happened impact your thoughts, words and actions. Not forgiving is palpable and felt in your body (your heart, your tummy, your shoulders), which is the barometer of your emotions. Really, do you still want to hold your Ex in your body? Erm… no!

I just want to finish by saying we all need to be forgiven at times in our lives, and learning a little forgiveness can go a long way towards making life a little easier and kinder – and boy, do we need to feel the kinder, softer times during divorce and relationship breakups!

Making Loneliness Your Friend

Let's not kid ourselves here, at some point in your separation and divorce – whether you instigated it or not – you will feel lonely. This is usually accompanied with varying degrees of isolation, fear and sadness – bad, right? Unfair too on top of everything else!

We're going in 'deep' in this section, feeling into and discovering some inner peace along the way, so trust me and bear with…

American professor Brené Brown wrote about 'true belonging' as a practice of 'believing in and belonging to yourself' in such a way that

*you share yourself with the world so you are
part of something, even when you're alone.*

It's powerful to actually come to the place where you're okay with yourself, where you are your own best friend and where you find inner peace. You are the one who most has your own back. Consider the possibility that who you are is all that you need to belong in this crazy world.

Let's talk FOMO (the crippling Fear of Missing Out)

Have you ever clicked on social media and FOMO slaps you round the chops, karate kicks you in the gut and hands you the comparison first-prize trophy of 'sad, unloved and lonely person'? We know many human beings live on their lonesome; literally millions around the globe wanting to connect as friends, lovers, to be loved, hugged, smiled at and spoken to. With FOMO, our first thought is to seek others to escape loneliness and replace it with 'togetherness' – it is in our nature. If you were in a lonely marriage, did you think one day the loneliness might go away? It didn't, right? And did you think divorce would sort it? What I learned was that getting this loneliness thing sorted begins with (you guessed it) ourselves.

Talking about loneliness with clients results in either a super-quiet pause or a glorification of busyness. Whatever place a client comes from, they usually end up in tears. It's a tough but important conversation and needs to be talked about or you just end up avoiding it, and loneliness continues to rent space in your head.

Wouldn't it be so cool to literally turn it around so you became the natural antidote and remedy for your loneliness? (Take a read of my blog post 'Is Divorce Lonely Better Than Married Lonely?' on the Divorce Goddess link in the Resources section.)

Changing FOMO to JOMO (the glorious Joy of Missing Out)

Returning to an empty house, without your children in tow, would have most marrieds literally jumping for joy pre-divorce. But when you're not given the choice, it feels a lot harder. This is when the DMMs get busy, digging up all those FOMO experiences in your life and then unkindly handing them to you like a toxic cocktail as soon as you walk through your front door.

On her 'Mum's weekend off', instead of seeing friends or going out, Lucy would close her curtains, curl up on the sofa, eat little, binge on Netflix, wine and weekend fags until it was time to get herself together and pick her kids up. She said she got so sick of punishing herself for having 'failed' at her marriage, feeling guilty about wasted time and her lack of mental and emotional strength to 'get out there' that she knew she had to do something. I introduced her to the story of the two arrows (see 'Resisting the pull of social media' in Chapter 2, but a quick reminder: the first arrow is the painful event – something we can't always control; the second arrow is if we inflict more pain upon ourselves, which is optional). She began to notice when she reverted to 'self-inflicted pain'. We put a supportive plan of action together to challenge the DMMs that sent her into 'that dark place' that included a self check-in ("How am I doing?") with three options to choose from when she felt wobbly: a long walk with her neighbour's dog, booking in to see a friend, or a mastery activity like clearing out a cupboard or cooking herself a nutritious new dish (see the later section in this chapter, 'Mastery activities', for more on this). Lucy began to make wiser choices that supported her mental and emotional health and helped with her loneliness.

So how can you resist picking up the second arrow, which may include 'Norman no mates' thoughts where you sink into shame, self-loathing and other unhelpful states?

See being alone as the opportunity to get your 'ducks in a row'! This is your time to get to know yourself, spoil yourself and do all those things you've been wanting to learn, make, sort… to tick things off the list of infinite possibilities waiting for you and change how you see this time so you can embrace, love and live the f*ck out of it!! This is your life, so if you're regularly putting it on hold and feeling sorry for yourself – come on, you know deep down you're stronger and better than that!

It's all about planning and balance, flexibility and self-kindness.

Try this: I put a shout out to my Instagram followers and here are some of the suggestions other lovely divorcees came up with about how to deal with loneliness and embrace JOMO...

- Put loud music on and sort, clean and do the jobs that you know need to be done and that when they're done you'll feel good – mastery activities (explained in more detail a little later)!
- Learn a new skill/recipe/language: no excuses with online courses at very little cost.
- Make a plan for your weekends to include people to see and speak to, a trip out on your own somewhere – even to buy ice cream to eat later while bingeing on a TV series.
- Buy a sex toy and use it – start loving your OWN body.
- Get brave, join an online or in-person group and get yourself out there – paddle-boarding, hiking, boxing (Thai kickboxing worked for me!) or a book club – we have no excuses! And if you're stuck, choose something you've never done – say goodbye to comfort zones and all that – see your divorce as a fresh opportunity and outcool yourself!

- Speaking of cool – well, mostly frickin' freezing – go find a cold water swim group! This was my choice – it's free, you feel AMAZING afterwards and it washes away those divorce life 'wobbles'.

Emma had been frightened all her life of cold water. Since separating from her Ex, she had decided to embrace each and every opportunity to go beyond her fears. 'Feel the post-separation fear and do it anyway' was her new mantra. After her first sea swim, in between laughing, Emma said, "I can't remember feeling so elated in such a long time and the rush of adrenaline made me feel like I was alive again! I felt I had left in the seawater so many emotions I was holding on to."

- Go to the cinema or a restaurant and notice others are on their own too! Stop caring what anyone else thinks. How can you even know what they think? (The first time I went to a restaurant on my own I got chatted up by a seriously good-looking guy – *win win* – fortune favours the brave, I say…)
- Go on holiday with yourself or a group, book and just bloody get on that plane! We don't ALWAYS need a Thelma or Louise alongside us! Had I not, I wouldn't have

gone for a swim with a fit and very available 26-year-old at 51 years old, nor sat naked on a nudist beach with an also naked male gay couple laughing our heads off, or got to hang out with myself writing chapters of this book with a glass of wine at sunset.

So, get out of your zone of alone, stop being a victim (you hate this, I know!) and best-friend yourself.

Try this: Let's get on this loneliness thing!

- Begin by writing down everything you hate about loneliness. Getting your fears down on paper often reduces them as you can see clearly that they're not always as bad as the DMMs make them out to be. Remember, no more picking up that second arrow and stabbing yourself.
- Next, write down everything that being on your own affords you – get creative and be wild. Use these lists to utilise the time you have, to plan ahead and also accept when you feel sh*t – it's okay to do so, it's about taking those small steps forward!

Jon had felt lonely in his marriage for many years. He realised children, life and work had got in the way of his time with his wife Ruth and he ended up having an affair. He avoided conversations and drank on his own each night watching porn, an escape he hated. After his affair came out, and a lot of couples counselling, they separated. As he sat in his flat, Jon realised that he still felt lonely. He realised the answer to his feeling lonely was actually all about him, and numbing these feelings with avoidance activities – TV, porn, social media and dating apps – was increasing his sense of separation rather than sorting it.

We worked on Jon getting to know himself first by trying meditation. Meditation was scary for Jon; he imagined all sorts of stuff could come up for him when he closed his eyes and sat still in a quiet space. We started with guided meditations, rather than just silence, and that helped him a lot. Jon would meditate when he felt the loneliness monkeys creeping up. He said whereas before, hearing his colleagues' weekend plans, he'd sink into a 'lonely hole' of shame, pity and sadness, he now goes to the bathroom to spend a couple of minutes focusing on his breathing, which helps him come back from his difficult thoughts. He realised that learning to be with himself rather than finding solace elsewhere was key and until he came to accept that he was okay to hang out with himself, the feelings of loneliness would always be there.

So next time loneliness comes knocking, check in with yourself. Treat it like a barometer of how you're feeling, and what self-care practices you need to revisit. Try to welcome it in, sit with it, make it tea, and be happy to see it because you know it's not forever, but an indication of where you're at and what you're going through.

Finding Balance

For many years I prided myself on being the '100 miles an hour' person who could balance many plates: mothering, cooking, cleaning, working, wife-ing, friending, socialising... the list goes on. I laughed at people for saying they could only focus on one thing at a time.

What I realised going into my divorce is this: the more plates I tried to spin, the more exhausted I became. Plate spinning is a random, mentally unhealthy way to live and when the plates fall, we beat ourselves up. Divorce is fertile ground for reducing self-worth and self-confidence, and we can end up shaming ourselves unkindly for not getting loads done or 'doing' life well. Remember, it may be that neither you nor your Ex have ever had to spin the divorce plates before. Applying kindness to the life practice of plate spinning is about getting clever with what we need to focus on first. It's about finding peace, exercising good self-care and taking the pressure off ourselves, regularly recharging our batteries, choosing to drop a couple of plates and trusting ourselves more.

One day, during my divorce, after I dropped my children off at school, I made a cup of tea and started crying for no reason. I didn't stop for six hours and sought refuge in the very small downstairs bathroom. I sat on the floor and wept, in overwhelm, seriously stressed and exhausted with holding it all together. It was the day of reckoning that I won't ever forget and still is my 'forever' benchmark as to when I'm spinning too wildly and need to take everything down a notch and help myself.

Finding balance is about growing your awareness with regular check-ins as to how you're feeling, and not overriding your body when it's begging you to rest because you're knackered with thoughts such as "I've got to get through this no matter what" or "I'll relax at the end of the day" and then not giving yourself a rest. Life is too precious to be thinking of the future when you live in Cortisol Land. You need the happy hormone dopamine to offset, rebalance and recharge your batteries; this is what rediscovering balance is all about.

How do you actually find the energy to get balance, while living through separation and divorce? No matter how much we try to control life, part of finding balance is accepting that life presents us with bumps in the road: some bigger and uglier than others. Building your resilience muscle through your divorce is key to managing these times by creating a daily (or most days – I'll let you off) habit like meditation (see my free Taster Mindfulness & Meditation Course link in the Resources section), journaling, self-kindness and gratitude. These are all foundations to help you keep the most important plates in the air and for you to consciously put the others down, if only for the moment.

Try this: Make a conscious effort to stay present and do your best to focus 100% during the tasks you do each day:

- When you're washing up, notice the sound of the water, feel the squish of the sponge and pay close attention to getting each piece clean.
- If you're listening to your child talking about every detail about their weekend with your Ex, really listen to your child; be present and available; connect with what they're going through and ensure they know you're listening.
- When you're out exercising, connect to your body – become aware of the miracle of what this body of yours can do, push yourself a little further, then celebrate that you did!

In essence, make this your best divorce day by giving everything you're doing your full attention – including looking after yourself. This may look like drinking your whole cup of tea (while it's hot) rather than a couple of sips, stretching your body after time at your desk, or getting engrossed in a book.

Try this: Write down any specific actions or thoughts that made a huge difference to how you felt. Finding balance is observing what makes you feel great and then doing it again until it becomes a positive daily habit. So, if your child was more open about their weekend experience because they knew you were really listening – what a win that is, yes?

While this seems so simple, focusing your mind on daily tasks is a great way to train your divorce mind monkeys (DMMs) to do what you want them to do rather than letting them run your show, which ultimately leads to bad plate spinning, overwhelm, conflict and less balance.

Asking for help

Balancing everything is exhausting, mentally, emotionally and physically – so take a look at your list of loved ones (refer to 'Telling Those You Love' in Chapter 1) and consider who you can ask for help. Perhaps your children can get involved with a duster, hoover or by emptying the dishwasher – trust that they can do it and help them feel empowered by their effort. If the jobs don't get done so well and you feel a creeping sense of frustration – LET IT GO! Take a breath or take ten! Ask a grandparent to mind the children so you get time for divorce paperwork, or ask a friend who's good with numbers if you're struggling with your accounts.

Asking for help can be difficult, especially when we feel stressed or not worthy of help. We can sometimes forget that people love being asked for help – it makes them feel useful and makes your life easier. It's also being kind to yourself, so next time someone offers just say yes! Remember, you don't have to do everything on your own! Plus, when you feel better, it benefits those around you including your kids, who will be grateful for a less stressed parent.

Balancing yourself

It's easy to get caught up in all the things we have to do as a single parent and so often the temptation is to think that 'when we do all of *this*, we will feel more of *that*'. We overload ourselves, feel the pressure and end up feeling out of balance. It's then easy to get into the habit of procrastination and begin to avoid what we need to be looking at. Procrastination is fear in the form of stopping yourself, which is definitely not self-care, so remember: fear is not your boss.

Helen had been overwhelmed for a long time. "It was such a relief to have a realistic plan, accountability and to start small, chunking down my to-do list into manageable bite-sized tasks! I was less tired, could see the wood for the trees and I could do more of what made me happy rather than focusing on what didn't. The children noticed too, as they got more quality time with me.

Being out of balance can be tiring, especially if you've been putting off divorce jobs – like getting your financials in order, researching professionals or struggling to commit to a self-care practice (see the next section). Finding balance is about motivation, commitment and focus. Like all muscles, it requires strengthening with daily practice. Build slowly, steadily and chunk it down; save yourself from those painful days and you'll begin to notice changes in how you're feeling sooner.

Try this: If a friend was spinning too many plates, what would you suggest to them? Would you tell them not to beat themselves up for not getting it all right? Would you help them identify which plates they can drop or delegate? Would you use unkind, harsh and judgey words? Finding balance is also being gentle with the expectations and words you use about yourself.

Self-Care

*If you're not kind to yourself, how can you
expect anyone else to be kind to you?*

Self-care can be hard to find the time for, especially when going through a divorce. So often I hear clients say that it's another thing on their list and they'll get round to it. Without pointing out the huge white elephant in the room – saying it isn't doing it, right?! Don't get me wrong, we've all been there, falling into bed at the end of another day thinking, "I'll start tomorrow" until you land with an almighty thump, leaving you with a wellbeing headache bigger than you thought was possible.

If the whole concept of self-care feels beyond you right now, here's a gentle nudge to say *please* try. In this section we'll explore how you can change the words you use about yourself, and how, when you notice you're stressed, you have options to hand to support you to feel better and get life stuff done – all good steps towards a more peaceful you.

Words

Telling yourself you 'should' isn't helpful, and frankly I believe writing the word 'should' on a piece of paper and burning it is a great way to release yourself from the power this word has over you. Not only is this a releasing practice but it may also take you out of your comfort zone, and it's a declaration of war to anything not in alignment with where you want to be heading.

Lucy, a client who was an artist, spent her life apologising for being 'stupid' and 'an idiot'. She said she couldn't stop doing it. "I've done it for years; my Ex would always say I was clumsy, forgetful and an 'airhead', which was fine when I was young and didn't much care about anything other than putting oil on a canvas. But what I've realised through my divorce is that I'm also good at financials and organising, but just never gave myself credit for the positives. Once I stopped using negative words about myself, it was a lovely feeling."

If this sounds familiar, you're not alone. Over time, it's easy to lose our sense of self-worth, confidence and become what Lucy called 'a shadow of my former self'.

Try this: Notice if you're using unhelpful words or phrases about yourself throughout the day (whether out loud or in your head as self-talk), such as:

- I'm so stupid
- I've let everyone down
- I hate myself

- I'm so weak

- My life's a mess

- I'm such a failure

- I feel so helpless

- I feel invisible

- I'm so lazy

- I can't do this anymore

So much unkindness to yourself, right? No wonder you're not feeling so good. After reading this list, notice how you feel. Joyous and happy or sad and low? If you're saying words like this to yourself on a regular basis, are you able to see how they can fuel your lack of self-worth, further damage your confidence, and keep you small and disempowered?

Next, repeat the following words and notice if you feel differently:

- I am strong and I will get through this

- I've got this because I remember I am brave

- I'm doing okay taking one day at a time

- I have my own back and I'm in my power

- I can do this; I didn't choose anything I couldn't handle

- I love and respect myself for showing up for me

- I am focusing on making things right

Try this: Spend a few moments writing down alternative 'encouraging statements' or 'positive affirmations'. Get curious, creative and have some fun – celebrate who you really are! As you grow your awareness self-care muscle, try to notice when you're being unkind to yourself and resist. Self-care, like self-kindness, becomes a habit and it begins with you!

Actions

Many years ago I was introduced to the concept of pleasurable and mastery activities and I loved it right away. Firstly, it gave me permission to create a list of stuff that I could do for me – permission is a big one, right? And, secondly, it allowed me to look at the stuff I needed to get done and flip it as a positive rather than a negative neural pathway of 'another thing to do'.

Permission granted for the following!

Pleasurable activities

How does the word 'pleasurable' sound to you? Sit with this word – what images, thoughts and other words come to mind? Going through what you're going through, you might not feel you deserve pleasure or have time for it.

We want to change that, right? So, how can you introduce more pleasurable activities into your life?

Annabel said, "As soon as Tosh said 'pleasurable', I thought 'vibrator'! I realised that instead of hanging on for the needle in the haystack chance of a perfect date and great sex, I could actually have fun with me instead and not be disappointed!"

Try this: Spend some time imagining and feeling into the activities in your life that help you feel calmer, rested and recharged; those that nourish you, and give you energy and joy. They may be things like:

- Having a bath –in the middle of the day for a decadent feel; my kind of bath!
- Reading a book that you've wanted to read for EVER!!
- Sitting in a chair in the sun or going for a walk – just getting outside in the fresh air!
- Calling a friend who makes you laugh.
- Making a lovely meal for yourself.
- Cycling.
- Buying a bunch of flowers – for yourself.
- Dancing around your kitchen like no one's watching – who cares anyway?!
- Going cold water swimming.

If you feel that being kind to yourself will be in any way detrimental to you holding up through all of this, then you need self-care more than ever. So make it happen.

Catherine started crying when we looked at what she did to nourish herself. She said she realised that she hadn't even had a bath in the last three months. "I'm literally on it from the moment my eyes open and divorce life crashes in; I grab a quick shower and the day continues in this way. I fall into bed every night thinking "I got through another day". I've dreamed of having a bath, but never stopped to think – why not run one this evening? I feel I'm just functioning and if I stop and be kind to myself, I think I will crumple. Writing a list of these activities reminds me to not only look after myself but also to do them!"

Mastery activities

These are the parts of our lives that we need to do, or are the 'needful' (love that word) that we don't think we have the headspace or inclination to do and yet, when they're done, we feel great that we did them!

Try this: Write yourself a list of everything you 'need' to do, and here are some suggestions from me:

- Organising the black hole of the house – perhaps the understairs cupboard that depresses the crap out of you with all the stuff thrown in there
- Sorting out the garden – mowing the lawn, planting pots of flowers and veg and making it a lovely outside space (no matter how small)
- Creating a gorgeous bedroom; make this your loving, nurturing, safe and inviting space, clear out what you need to and love being in there
- If your email inbox depresses the hell out of you each time you open it, gift yourself (believe me, this is a gift) an hour to get rid of, say, 500 messages!
- Doing your divorce documents and paperwork, getting more organised

Try this: Write your Pleasurable and Mastery lists out and stick them where you'll regularly look at them to remind you that you can lift yourself out of that slump, stop those difficult thoughts and get through the days. And if all else fails, buy ice cream and try the following practice.

Ice Cream Indulgence: If you're going to eat ice cream, please use it as an opportunity to practise self-care so you feel less guilty! Plus, children love this activity so try it with them!

- Get brave and choose a new flavour. Remove the wrapping and before you dive in (I'm assuming the whole tub is in your hand, or, if you're behaving, you have some scoops in a bowl), pause and look at the ice cream closely. Observe the texture and colours; spend a few moments letting your eyes soak up every detail.

- Now take in the smell. Is it strong or subtle? Notice what's happening in your mouth. Are you salivating as you anticipate the experience of eating it? Can you stay with the anticipation for a few moments longer, noticing the feelings in your body or the DMMs screaming "eat it!"?

- Taste the first spoonful. What are the sensations of the cold ice cream meeting the warmth of your mouth? Feel the sensations of melting and the different flavours released as the ice cream dissolves – be like an ice cream advert on the beach!

- Resist the temptation to swallow the ice cream and gulp down another mouthful. Instead, let the flavour and sensations linger, and only when you feel you've fully experienced all that this spoonful has to offer should you swallow it. Enjoy all the flavours and smells, and the play of warmth and cold in your mouth as you take another mouthful and let it linger. Carry on repeating this until you finish your ice cream (well, maybe not the whole tub). How do you feel, is it different from normal? Did the ice cream taste better eating it this way? You might want to consider this a meditation!

Whether you are mindfully eating an ice cream, clearing out a cupboard or luxuriating in a bath, accessing peace is really about taking control of the DMMs so you have full ownership of your actions rather than being beholden to old habits, exhaustion-induced reactions, and fight, flight and freeze divorce fog decisions.

While it feels a million miles away from where you are now, know this: it does get better the more you stay present with what's happening, be it driving through beautiful countryside to drop the kids off, finding a way through a difficult conversation or appreciating being in a quiet house.

You have everything already within you to achieve peace. And you were born with a kind heart; tap into your lovely heart and know you are powerful, and you can access the power already within you when you need to. Remind yourself often of this and make it something you say to yourself each day in the mirror;

words and intentions are powerful and even when you feel disempowered, know you can always begin again. More opportunities come for us to find peace when we apply kindness to conflict. You saying "yes" to a more compassionate way of being is like a big flag to the universe of conflict that says "Yes, I'm doing the work so bring it on!" Keep doing the work; trust and believe it is all there for your personal development during this time.

Which leads us on to Chapter 4 – joy and happiness, laughter and fun, and everything else that makes you smile!

Chapter 4

Feeling Joy

Can you imagine feeling true joy again? Perhaps this seems like a daft question – but it's important! In the depths of the dark nights of your divorce, you may say otherwise. It can feel like you have nothing left and your little fire has gone out, reduced to an ember – trust me, I have the T-shirt! What we forget in these times though is that we have a choice; we can choose whether to open up to the joy that is out there in the world – no matter how small – or stay caught up in the rumblings of negativity.

If you find yourself saying, "When this divorce is over, I'll feel happier and more joyful," then accessing that wonderful feeling of joy is always on the premise that something has to happen first (the end of your divorce, in this case). Living in this way means joy never has permission to be in your daily present moment – your 'now' life.

You can change this. In this chapter, I will give you a beautiful life pass for you to feel joy every day, with simple tools, practices and habits you can try. You have a sovereign right, no matter what you are going through, to feel joy.

I will share with you how to grow your joy by:

- Recognising joy and growing your joy awareness muscle
- Knowing it's okay to have a sh*tty day when you hit unexpected bumps in the road
- Accepting your divorce and letting go of the pain
- Moving obstacles to happiness out of the way
- Embracing the power of gratitude
- Looking after and loving your body

How Do I Feel Joy?

There's a loaded question! First, are you ready to feel joy? Do you spend your days looking at the smiles of everyone else and wondering what it would feel like to be there again, in that space? Is joy something that you secretly don't think you'll be able to feel while going through a divorce – that everyone else is able to access but you? If so, we need to change your habits.

Sometimes, when we want something so badly, it almost stays away – as if we're blocking it. Call it the Law of Attraction (more on that in the section 'A little on the Law of Attraction' in Chapter 6). It's like when you're feeling lonely as f*ck and nobody calls or messages, until you say, "F*ck it! I'm okay on my own" – and then the messages and calls come rolling in.

Feeling joy is not conditional, it's about getting out of your mind and back into your heart to allow it to come in, to see it every day and grow the neural muscle that, with exercise, gives you immediate access to joy whenever you need it. Joy is a balm – the salve that softens the divorce wounds and edges; the more you apply, the better you feel. Even a small dose of joy can make all the difference.

Understand what works for you

Checking in with what does and what doesn't work for you enables you to make those ever-so-slight adjustments to keep you on track. When we fall into 'kindness complacency', this can cause your joy battery to go flat, leading to conflict. It's easy to take your eye off the kindness ball when you've had a great week, month or day, but this is where conflict can sneakily rear its head and surprise you as the joy battery starts to run out. Just as you're getting comfortable, the potential for conflict appears, like that Friday solicitor's letter that lands on your doormat. You pick it up and open it without thinking. You realise too late it's going to be something you wish you hadn't looked at until Monday morning, and you feel the emotional gut punch of the contents throughout the weekend. If you're caught like this, choose to see it as a learning opportunity rather than a failing. Flip it so it becomes a positive – a reminder to not ruin your weekend by opening the letter early or without preparing yourself, which is a nod to taking deep breaths so your DMMs don't send you spiralling downwards.

Or perhaps you've had a great week and you're on cloud nine, looking forward to your weekend off, until you find out your Ex is no longer able to have the children and your excitement plummets (think a balloon and pin – POP!). Life doesn't always go to plan and this would be an easy time to lose your focus on kindness in divorce, but try to turn this into a positive and find joy in the extra time with your children. Don't let your disappointment rob you of the joy of being able to hug your children more, slum it in pyjamas with them, and bake and eat cookies while cosied up together on the sofa.

Perhaps a date or dinner with friends gets postponed and you face the weekend in rather than out. Look at what you can do to fill the time – flip your thoughts and go straight into positive mode, rather than falling into victim mode and experiencing low self-worth. Use it as an opportunity to celebrate increasing the power of you rather than diminishing it – have a luxe bath, read that book you bought ages ago, meditate or clean your house. You have a choice: do NOT let the DMMs push you into that neural pathway of negativity; instead, own your weekend and make it fully yours.

Or maybe, after a long hard slog at your financials, you discover your Ex is still stuck doing theirs. Celebrate that you have done yours rather than disappearing into that rabbit hole about why they didn't do theirs in good time. Focus on you, flipping what happens every day/week to finding the positive!

Try this: Take a moment to think about how you can change the way you see stuff (like your Ex's difficult behaviour) and turn it into something more joyous:

- What brings me joy and how can I increase this feeling? (Maybe focusing on the future of not being in a marriage with them, for starters!)
- What doesn't bring me joy and how can I flip it so it works for me? (Perhaps, if you expect your Ex to be late for pick-ups, you could transform this into being grateful for the extra time to talk to the kids or check emails?)
- What can stay that brings me more joy? (Maybe celebrating the clarity of what you do and don't want that you realise and appreciate by having difficult people in your life?)
- What cannot stay? (Perhaps holding resentment and anger inside around your Ex – you get to choose if this stuff stays or goes?)

Now look at the list and write three (or more if you wish) things under each of the questions. Maybe you can identify some old habits that don't bring you joy, like going to a gym that you hate rather than running outside; paying for a dating app you're not ready for; drinking on weekdays; clothes you don't enjoy wearing anymore; or hating where you're working rather than finding another job. You might also commit more to habits that are meaningful to you and bring you joy, such as only keeping what you love in your home; changing the location of the kids' pick-up/drop-off so it's a nicer place for you all (rather than settling for a service station that reminds you of your parent's divorce…); or wearing more yellow (if you can!).

Look at your list every day until you're ready to be courageous and take action to make joyful changes to your life. Write them on a sticky note and pop it on your bathroom mirror so you're reminded at least twice a day of your commitment to take action. Then, commit to making at least one of these actions happen this week.

Starting to clear away what doesn't give you joy is like saying "yes" to joy to come into your life. No one's up there in the gods saying, "You don't deserve joy today." We have to walk wholeheartedly and bravely into the energy of joy so we can clear out what doesn't bring us joy.

Get creative and enjoy the process of taking these steps to help you feel empowered and more confident, and begin to focus on what works for you (and brings you joy) – and what doesn't!

Try this: Here are some ways you might flip your behaviours to bring more joy into each day:

- Put your favourite playlist on when doing household chores rather than having the radio on in the background.
- Wear what you love each day – don't wait to wear what you love!
- Water the garden in the morning if you're too tired in the evening.
- Drive or walk a slightly different way to work or school, and celebrate how beautiful nature is.
- Smile and say hello to strangers if you are out, or have a conversation with people you don't know – there's so much loneliness in the world, so make someone's day (and yours!).
- Practise gratitude by being thankful for three people who have made a positive difference to your day.
- Clear up the children's toys and sing – let your children see their parent in full funniness!
- Take off your social media notifications!

Focus on what you love, can change and want to do more of. Accept that parts of your day may feel more joyous than others depending upon how you're feeling – for example, ask yourself: "Am I hungry, angry, ill, lonely or tired?" If any of these applies, is it making a difference to how you react or does it provide you with a different lens through which you see your experience? Remember: you have a choice about your life – to feel more joy by doing more of what *brings* you joy!

Grow your awareness

A great way to feel joy is to become the observer in your own life: to get into the habit of taking a step back and seeing it from above. What is the situation or person saying to you? What can you do to change how you see what is happening and say "yes" to joy?

Take divorce – if you were to say to yourself, "This is an opportunity to grow my resilience and strength; to learn and discover more about myself," rather than staying in victimhood forever at the mercy of your thoughts, words and actions around your Ex, then you are bringing in the energy of joy. To better illustrate this, take a couple of moments to close your eyes and think about how it would feel to be optimistic rather than pessimistic. Where do you feel this in your body? Is there a sneaking chance in hell you could choose to be positive over negative?

It's hard sometimes, especially as we tend to focus on the more negative aspects of life and we're more likely to remember the bad experiences rather than the good.

Alex was a perfect example. He said, "My life is sh*t. I don't see my children, I don't see anyone, I don't have any money, my life is really sh*t."

Alex was choosing to see his whole life as a total mess – which, let's be honest, is easy in Divorceville. It may be that there were elements of his life that were in a mess. Take the example of someone saying "My back hurts." When you ask them where it hurts, they point and say, "This bit down here…" but that's not all of their back, right? If you adjust the lens from which you're viewing your life, you're better able to take control of the catastrophising DMMs.

After delving deeper during a coaching session, Alex realised:

- He did see his children through a well-balanced parenting plan, just not as much as he had done when he had been married.
- He saw his friends on weekends for cycling; he just didn't have the family noise around him all the time when he was at home anymore, which at times he was grateful for.

- Alex didn't have as much money as he once had, but he still had enough to save, rebuild his life and treat his children – and also himself.
- His life wasn't "sh*t", he just needed to grow his awareness, find those precious glimmers of light and bank the joy that he felt when they appeared.

You are not your divorce mind monkey thoughts.

It's Okay to Have a Sh*tty Day

Let's not skirt around this one. Sh*tty days are real and, divorce or no divorce, they're out there waiting to drop into our lives at a moment's notice. What might seem to be a beautiful day ahead can turn at the drop of a hat to pee all over your fireworks, sometimes with surprising ease! These days can sometimes start at 4.30am or mark the end of an otherwise beautiful day (think late for pick-up/drop-off).

Working with how we react to these days is the difference. When the next one lands in your life, it's an opportunity to be with the experience, understand why it has happened and prescribe yourself your best remedy – whether it is creating a supportive plan to get through your day (maybe by postponing meetings, eating good comfort food or setting an alarm to check in with yourself every couple of hours) or, failing that, having a cosy 'bed' day.

A sh*tty day doesn't happen because you failed to be 'Up' all of the time (feeling nourished and full of joy). Sometimes it's important to accept that you can also be 'Down' (feeling down and depleted) – and that's okay. These bumps in the road are useful reminders to appreciate the good stuff that you can gain from them (like resilience, grit and strength) – it's normal and part of being human!

On the days when all you can do is brush your teeth, dump last night's wine bottle into the recycling, clean up after the children and get to work, think of this: everyone is going through stuff that you know nothing about – you are not alone. Although it's tempting to sugar-coat what's happening with "I'm fine", it's also okay to say, "I'm not having a great day, but tomorrow it may be better!"

Stating this belief plants a seed in your unconscious mind, which you can water as you go through your day and through your divorce. Think of those incredible plants that grow out of unyielding concrete slabs – and they still flower. Good days, bad days – bring them all in, be with them, find the small joys in where you are and know that today is not where you will be forever. It is just for today.

If nothing else, at least you can name your sh*t day and perhaps give whoever you're speaking to permission to have a sh*t day too (they may appreciate it more than you realise!). The world is full of sh*t days and it just so happens that one landed on you today. To feel more empowered, you could simply say to yourself, "I'm doing a sh*tty day today", thereby owning it!

Owning it is also about self-kindness. If you're going into a meeting or you've overcommitted yourself, can you reschedule or share with people that this isn't a great day? It takes the pressure off you, but it also shows that you have the courage to be honest. It's a layer of kindness that can benefit everyone involved, especially you. There's nothing more healing than facing days like this rather than sweeping them under the carpet and pretending they don't exist – believe me, it just gets harder to face them next time. Being present with your sh*tty days helps you understand why they sneak up; you get to know their triggers, too, so you can manage the experience with more self-kindness, such as by reducing alcohol or social media, doing more exercise, meditating, or eating better.

Try this: Think about a sh*tty day you've experienced and write down what it looked like to you. Think about the following:

- Who was involved (just you, your Ex, your family, your friends, strangers)?
- What did you/they say?
- How did you/they act?
- What were you thinking/what do you think they were thinking?

There are always going to be times when you just want to stay under the duvet, whether the sun is shining or it's grey and rainy outside. Accepting these times is part of life, but it's not your whole life. Life isn't linear and you're not a failure for feeling like this; instead, you can see this moment as an opportunity to look a little deeper at why you feel the way you feel, what makes you feel like this, and how you can make small changes towards feeling better on the bad days.

At one point I went to my doctor to talk about antidepressants. I had been on them for the last three years of my marriage and came off them just before separating, and after lots of days where I felt like the proverbial, I booked an appointment. I spoke about what I was going through and asked if I needed them. This lovely doctor simply said, "It's no surprise you're feeling as you are, you're going through a lot of really tough stuff but it's not going to be forever." He gave me permission to feel the way I did, which helped me understand that I could manage what was happening in my life at that time.

This advice was specifically for me and not for everyone. If you're feeling like you really cannot cope, do go and seek professional advice. Please don't feel ashamed – put on your brave pants and ask.

It's okay not to be okay

The hardest days may come crashing down upon you simply as a result of someone pulling out in front of you on the road, the children playing up or you feeling unwell. How you choose to get through the day is for you to decide. Talking to friends about a bad day may help you feel better initially, but it's still helpful to look at why you're feeling the way you are and how you can help yourself. For example, consider this: when you talk about something negative, does the energy grow or does it dissipate? I personally find that talking about something bad a lot doesn't make me feel better – quite the opposite.

Maybe you wake up one day and for no apparent reason, the heaviness of your divorce descends upon you like a thick, unreasonable blanket. Or perhaps you've arranged to see friends, who for no apparent reason have cancelled, leaving you with no reason to get out of the house at the weekend. Your energy feels robbed and you feel that aching kick in the gut as the negative thoughts and feelings hit you hard.

Notice what *your* triggers are that make your days feel difficult – maybe it is feelings of loneliness, or perhaps it will help to revisit the questions in the 'Managing Conflict' section of Chapter 3 (so you can understand more about your triggers).

Self-kindness is all about how you react or respond: to be kind or not kind; to beat yourself up or apply self-love. For example, if someone cancels plans on you, know that's okay, it's not always about you. Try to take yourself out of the 'poor me' way of thinking and instead consider what you can do to 'build yourself up'. Go on an adventure with just you, find the joy in being with yourself – wow, you're awesome! Get comfortable and remember that you're actually pretty cool to hang out with – and if you don't think you're good to hang out with, is that because of the energy you're putting out into the world?! Send those DMMs packing by replacing those doubting moments with the joy of being YOU!

Recalling joyful moments on darker days

Now, let's take a look at pleasant events. Even during a dark time in your life like divorce, you will also experience moments of joy throughout the week – and by becoming more aware of how you feel, you can bank the joyful experiences and refer back to them when everything feels difficult and joyless.

Try this: In Chapter 3, we looked at managing conflict and unpleasant events; here, we're going to do a similar exercise, this time looking at noticing the good stuff and pleasant events. Time to get clear on those moments of joy (and bank the feel-good vibes) that also happen during the week:

- What is the happy and joyous event?
- How does it make me feel?
- Where do I feel it in my body?
- How are my thoughts about it?
- How can I use it to remind me of the good stuff on sh*tty days?

Sarah found herself falling into a "pit of despair" when things didn't go as she'd planned. She sat with the questions and reviewed her week to remind herself of the good stuff that had happened so she could rationalise with the DMMs, which were screaming at her that her life was a series of unpleasant events and sh*tty days. She was able to see that, for the most part, her week had been good, and it was only on one day that something had happened that really wasn't so good. It was the reminder that she needed, and she began to recognise when she was slipping into the pit so she could take herself out of it.

When something pleasant or positive happens in your week, no matter how big or small, note it down in your notebook or journal so you can grow your awareness about how you act, think and how your body feels as a result. Get used to noticing how something lovely makes you feel so you can create a positive, 'go-to' neural pathway. What works for you and gifts you a moment of happiness? What did you do to increase the feelings of joy (which is a practice of self-kindness)? What can you use as a rebalancing tool (such as exercising or meditating, singing, or cooking nourishing food that you enjoyed with friends, or simply deciding to be more smiley to your Ex the next time you see them)?

Bringing it back to your Ex and your divorce, notice the relief and joy you feel when things go well: the unexpected positive email that allays your fears; the lovely night in with your children, sitting on the sofa and watching a film together while munching on popcorn; how good you feel when you visit houses that you could potentially buy/rent, and the hope that brings for your future.

Try this: Getting clear about what is good for you and what isn't helps to reaffirm that you do have some control over how you feel.

Draw three different-coloured circles inside each other labelled Red (outside), Yellow (next) and Green (in the centre), which range from what 'isn't' to what 'is' good for you. Each circle has space to write in different activities. Get clear in each space about what helps you feel joy and what doesn't. The following suggestions give examples of what is good and not great for you as you think about what to write in each circle:

- RED: Write down all the activities that almost always make you feel bad (such as social media, financial paperwork, pick-ups/drop-offs, seeing your Ex, binge drinking, eating too much chocolate, dating apps).

- YELLOW: Write what makes you feel good and sometimes bad depending on what is happening or how you are feeling (such as speaking to close friends who know your Ex, hanging out with marrieds, dating, social media, picking up/dropping off your kids). Maybe think about when you are HAILT – hungry, angry, ill, lonely and tired.

- GREEN: What brings you joy? What makes you feel great and increases your dopamine happy hormones? (It may be exercising, seeing friends or family, meditating, laughing, cold water swimming, singing, dancing…)

Becoming more aware is an easy win – it's putting the noticing into practice that takes consistent effort until it becomes something you're aware of naturally. Remember, you have a choice about what you do or how you prepare that can also contribute to a sh*tty day or make it easier to manage. Taking positive action supports you to manage the tougher days better, rather than doing the same unhelpful stuff over again, which leaves you feeling dreadful – and before you know it, you've had a terrible week, rather than just one day.

Acceptance Versus Holding On

Serenity prayer – the divorce version!

Universe, grant me the serenity to accept the things my Ex says, thinks and does that I cannot change, and the courage and strength to change the things I say, think and do, and for the wisdom for me to know this and make a difference.

Acceptance is about letting go of the stuff in your divorce and life that you KNOW deep inside isn't serving you. It's that lightbulb moment of revelation where you decide something isn't going to affect you so much because you're going to let it go. Acceptance is also about picking your battles and not running with the "I'm right and you're wrong" narrative, which, as we all know, isn't helpful and is instead guaranteed to inflame and cause conflict.

Holding on, on the other hand, feels 'graspy', desperate and fearful. When you hold on, you're less able to see a way through the problem or issue in front of you – you block your own way forward, it's as if you've put up a barrier to progress. You know that's not how you want to operate because you're stronger than that, even if you don't feel that way all the time.

Talking about acceptance and letting go is always an interesting conversation with clients. It's the one most likely to have them shuffling in their seats. This is good, because it's an indicator that they need to do some work on acceptance to stop them dragging the things they're holding on to into their future.

So what is acceptance and letting go, and why is it so important in divorce? It is a process of reducing (and healing) what you most hold onto that is a kicker, triggers you or depletes your energy. It stops you from lugging resentment, anger and other emotions into your future. The key to this is letting go of one small irritant at a time and trusting that when you do, you'll feel better. It doesn't make your Ex right, or you appear weak, but it's a route to feeling more joy if you're ready to commit and say yes to it. I know – so much work, right?! But when you have the courage to let go of what is not good for you or your future, you make way for more magic.

For many, they want to punish their Ex for the painful and selfish actions that led to the divorce. I'm not advocating on any level that acceptance means saying what your Ex did to you was right – acceptance isn't a waiver. However, it is a life opportunity – a chance for you to choose how you want to live your future life and what emotional baggage you want to drag around with you as you move forwards.

The two arrows story (refer to the section 'Resisting the pull of social media' in Chapter 2) again comes to mind – the first arrow being the pain of the divorce inflicted upon you, while the second arrow is what you decide to do with that pain. Do you want to carry it, hold it and feel it in every conversation or family event, and go to sleep with it for the rest of your life? Or would you prefer to put the second arrow down, learn from your experiences and honour your courage, and commit to healing the wound from the first arrow?

Louise shared during a session: "I can't forgive my husband for what he did. He left me after 35 years of marriage. I gave him everything – two children, my career, I supported him – and he left me for a woman five years older than our eldest son. I know my children want it to be okay so we can see each other at family events – it's so hard and I see it in their eyes – but they don't know my pain; they'll never know."

I felt this deeply; what I felt even more deeply was that this wonderful woman, who was so angry and hurting, knew on some level that to truly move on she had to face the undeniable truth that acceptance was what was going to set her free.

It's also not for the children to know the pain of a divorce – it is not about them. It is down to both their parents to make it okay for them, which is far better than the children having to navigate and tiptoe around their parents for the rest of their lives. They lost their family unit too.

I am a great believer in accepting the part we have to play in the experiences we have in life. We don't always get life right, but we have an opportunity to accept where we are – and if we show up well, with compassion and kindness, then this is enough. Accepting what feels good for us in life as opposed to holding on to the bad stuff is about choice, and we always have the choice to work with acceptance or stay holding on to that ledge, fearful of letting go. This knowledge helped Louise to understand she had control over her thoughts, words and actions, and it was an opportunity to grow out of holding her anger and feel more healed. The irony is the more we open ourselves to healing the part that we most fear, the less it hurts us going forwards.

The more you fight the need to accept and let go, the more it's going to hurt through your divorce and into your future. Holding on becomes a negative emotional store of revenge and anger, bitterness and grief, available to access when you feel low on self-esteem and disempowered. It is an open invitation to the DMMs to increase conflict within you. This can make you feel like a 'victim' (argggh, no!), indulge in the "I'm right and you're wrong" narrative or cite "the principle of the matter" (always dangerous, a family lawyer once told me).

Think of a friend who has been through a bad divorce. There may be conversations you avoid (perhaps you just don't want to hear it anymore or you feel the energy around the convo is negatively charged). And this is just how *you* feel about talking to them – can you imagine just how bad it feels for your friend to be carrying that negativity around inside them 24/7?

Realising this was a game-changer for me: someone I care about is still holding on so tightly to their anger and it makes me feel sad, and now it is so deep-rooted it may never leave.

Think of someone you know who is still holding on to their experience years after their divorce and isn't prepared to forgive and accept someone else's behaviour. How does this feel? Do you want this to be you in years to come? A male friend shared he was tired of dating beautiful women with big divorce settlements that had everything except peace in their hearts. This stuff sits inside you and can affect you finding love as you begin to move on.

Take the example of Keith, who felt such shame after being told by his wife that she wanted a divorce. He said it was uncomfortable for him, he hated himself for not being everything he thought she wanted. He said he couldn't look at his "abject failure"; it was too painful and it made him afraid of a future alone. We worked with his acceptance of what had happened so he could let go of what he thought had gone wrong rather than what had actually gone wrong, so he could feel at peace with his part in the ending of the marriage. He began to accept that carrying around shame wasn't going to help his confidence moving forwards or support him in finding another partner in the future.

Acceptance is a huge part of the healing process of a life event like divorce. As ever, there is a choice, and it's never too late to begin the process of letting go of what no longer serves you. Sometimes you don't know where to start or what to do to stop yourself from feeling judged, a failure and weighed down by what's happened to you. This is where a coach, therapist or counsellor can help you see the path through the murky world that is about holding on, rather than letting go.

So often, the conscious act of letting go can be a powerful support tool that helps release the blocks in your subconscious.

Try this: These activities may help you let go:

- Take a piece of paper and write down everything you want to forgive and can let go of, and then read it before burning it. If you want to get 'witchy', you can throw the piece of paper, along with lavender and rosemary from your garden, into a ceramic or metal pot and burn them together.

- Create a 'f*ck-it bucket'. Write down what you want to let go of and put the piece of paper into a cup or container. I've put many things into my f*ck-it bucket and let them sit in that energy. On checking the bucket every couple of months, it's interesting what's no longer a thing anymore! Have a go!

- Read or shout out what you're committing to letting go of from the top of your favourite mountain, on the beach or in your garden.

A lovely lady who I interviewed on the Divorce Goddess *podcast said she had some friends round for a ritual burning of her wedding dress, and on hearing this I thought "Ouch!" – but then she added they all wrote the good things about the marriage and her Ex on the dress before putting it on the fire. I liked this ritual a lot!*

Get Out of Your Own Way

The DMMs are our biggest block to having what we most want in life and feeling joy. We can see what we want and then there's this middle part that makes everything feel messed up, blocked and unobtainable – while frustratingly, we can see our perfect life just beyond and out of reach. We get into the habit of overthinking about how to get there, and our minds fill up with unhelpful, controlling and challenging thoughts. We start to sabotage ourselves, thinking we're not worthy enough to receive the good stuff in life. The more difficult the path ahead appears, the more we try to control what will happen, the more we procrastinate and prevaricate, the more we become avoidant, and it's a vicious cycle because things then get even harder – a bit like a divorce that's more about conflict than kindness. Self-kindness in divorce is growing your awareness so you can identify when this is happening and fully step in and overcome those DMM fears!

Here is a scenario that a client, Sam, found himself in: "Katie was always late in our marriage. I accepted that it was part of who she was; initially I found it entertaining, but towards the end it became what I can only describe as a massive irritant. Pick-ups and drop-offs were fertile ground for an argument and something I didn't want to have happen in front of the children. There was always some excuse. I wanted her to honour my time and commitment to being on time but I felt I had no control of her and her actions, which frustrated me more. One day I was waiting for her. I'd had a bad day at work and I'd ordered a coffee (that I knew would supercharge how I was feeling) and I kept looking at the clock every five minutes getting increasingly angry, she hadn't called and turned up 30 minutes late. I exploded; the children were upset, Katie was distressed and I felt angry and guilty. There wasn't one level on which this was good for any of us."

This story is by no means an uncommon one regarding timekeeping and co-parenting. A confession from me here is that, as someone who was not only notoriously late and also a child of divorced parents, I made a choice to always be early, not late, for my children. I had first-hand experience of just how difficult it is as a child to be in the middle of divorcing parents where one was always late and flustered and the other angry and sad.

When you no longer have control over your Ex, it can be difficult to get them to do anything. They don't need to do what you say – and they certainly won't behave as you'd hoped they would when you were married. Parents know this stuff is detrimental to their children, and yet so often still manage to make the source of conflict about each other (such as an Ex's bad timekeeping) and not the children. If you're in a position to see just what's going on and can make even a small change as to how you react, plus be a bigger person (even if your Ex is not), then please, for your children's sake, do.

Sam's Ex was late, she was not in any rush to change her timekeeping and she knew it bugged the crappola out of him, so she made her behaviour about Sam, not her children. Sam, while he hated what she was doing, realised he needed to manage his anger and emotions to protect his children by working on his stress levels. He made it about his children rather than trying to change his Ex.

What Sam found as a result of letting go of his expectations and trying to control Katie was that his energy changed. Then, almost as if she sensed her lateness was like water off Sam's back, Katie started being on time. She wasn't getting the rise from Sam, and she saw how her timekeeping stressed the children and how she looked bad from all sides. Call it a phenomenon, spookiness or the Universe at work, but the strangest things happen when we let go energetically – it's almost like things happen organically, by themselves. (Remember the example of the glass lamp bases in the section 'Sorting through your possessions' in Chapter 2.)

Take a moment to think about where things aren't working – in your divorce, co-parenting experience or any other area in your life. Notice how often you're thinking about the situation or the person involved, and the frustration, anger and difficult emotions that arise as a result, and check in with how you feel when you're in your own way – in other words, making things worse for yourself. Does your body tense up? Does your breathing become shallow or your voice change (for many people, their voices rise)? This isn't about judging your reactions but becoming more aware so you can see the effect that NOT getting out of your own way has on you and those you love.

You cannot shake hands if your fist is still clenched.

Alice said she had been waiting forever for her final divorce papers to come through; she noticed she felt stressed the more she wanted them to appear. We explored why she needed the papers on her time frame and she said, "Because I want them in my hands and for my divorce to be done, dusted and over with". We worked with the concept of her 'getting out of her own way'. Alice agreed to work on noticing the rising thoughts of 'wanting the papers' and letting the thoughts go, getting out of her own way and trusting that they would come through when they were meant to. Well, this stuff works because the next morning she received her Decree Absolute! Coincidence or serendipity? Whatever it is, this stuff works!

How is this concept sitting for you? I get that it may be a new way of thinking for you, and you may be sitting reading this and wondering if it works – but trust me. I cannot tell you the times I have done this – noticed when I want something so badly and it doesn't happen, then let go and got out of my own way to find that things 'seamlessly' happen. It's a bit like when you're trying to remember a word or name and it comes when you stop thinking about it!

Try this: If you're battling with one of your children or waiting and wanting your Ex to send you that email reply, work on accepting and letting go – and think about or move on to something else. Do it with an honest and open intention and trust it will happen without your intervention.

A final story on this I want to share with you belongs to me.

One grey autumn Sunday afternoon I decided to go for a run. The carpark was empty, bar one other car, and I was desperate to get out and run (early divorce days). Before I got out of the car I decided to leave my phone in it and stuffed my car keys into my pocket and started running. The curious thing is that I had my inner voice or gut instinct warning me to be careful. I was so desperate to run that I didn't listen. Thirty minutes in, I realised my car keys had fallen out of my pocket. This wood was in full autumn leaf-drop and there was no way I was going to find them; my phone was in the car and there was no one about. I started laughing; my gut instinct had tried to warn me, but I didn't listen. I needed this run so I decided to get out of my own way, continue running (even though the light was fading) and trust that it was going to work out – I just didn't know how. After another half an hour I started making my way back along the route, hoping divine intervention would happen and the keys would appear. It was a big call – there were a LOT of leaves. At a small intersection in the path, I met a couple who asked if I had lost my car keys. They had found my keys! What are the odds on this?

The Power of Gratitude

"Gratitude is the best attitude"
– Shamash Alidina

In divorce world, 'joy' can seem like breadcrumbs so it's important to collect them when we find them – and for me, this is what gratitude is all about.

Saying "Thank you" when you're in the middle of a divorce can feel kind of alien; saying "Thank you for all the sh*t that has happened and continues to happen" can feel even weirder. But if you want a kinder divorce, you can choose to integrate practices (such as gratitude) that support kindness for yourself, towards your Ex and towards those you love. Having a kinder divorce is all about doing things differently, challenging those DMMs and walking into what feels uncomfortable. In essence, gratitude has the power to magically humble us into a state of appreciation and thankfulness, and it goes some way to rebalancing the negative experience of divorce into a happier state.

Gratitude helps you discover how to want what you have, not want what you don't have. Divorce is the perfect time to introduce gratitude into your life, since you can feel as if everything you've ever wanted has been taken away from you in an instant (even though you may have spent at least some of the time in your marriage wanting what you didn't have or not wanting what you did have).

So, why is gratitude so important through your divorce? It has the power to transform everything: your perceptions, your experiences and your state of mind. If you've stumbled onto the divorce path with your rucksack full of heartbreak, treachery, resentment and fear, feeling grateful may not be the first destination you'd choose on the map. However, it is a tried-and-tested way to lighten your load – and instead of a stormy route ahead, you increase your chances of sunshine along the way.

The DMMs will tell you this practice sounds too simple to make a difference ("Saying thank you throughout your divorce? Yeah, right!"). But life doesn't always follow the path you expect it to, as your divorce may be showing you. When we spend our days desperately travelling to get somewhere else and focus on our future (rather than the present moment), we miss all the good stuff happening now – the in-between moments of happiness, joy and sunshine.

It's easy to become overwhelmed and get caught up in the negatives – gratitude changes this. We're less likely to go into victim mode, which in turn makes it easier for us to let stuff go and choose our battles more wisely.

Let's look at the science behind gratitude and how gratitude changes the brain.

Saying "Thank you" wakes up parts of your brain that are involved in feelings of reward (the reward is when stress is removed), so they support you to be a kinder divorcee – someone able to talk constructively with their Ex and be more open than closed to the idea of having a kinder divorce.

These areas of the brain also help to increase those all-important happy brain hormones, such as dopamine, serotonin and oxytocin. These hormones contribute to the feelings of happiness that come with gratitude.

I encourage you to build your gratitude muscle so your brain learns to tune into the positives. Instead of thinking, "Oh no, not another weekend on my own," you could think, "Great, I have so much time to do all those things I've been meaning to finish!" or you might turn "My Ex is never around enough for our children" into "I'm so grateful they have a father who's involved."

Flipping the norm to a new reality is supported by a daily gratitude process. If you find yourself focusing too much on the negative, gratitude is a simple way for you to nurture a more positive focus – teaching your brain and the DMMs to spend more time on the feel-good stuff and less time hanging on to the things that wear you down.

Try this: Instead of waking up and wanting to disappear under the duvet, decide to say thank you for what you have in your life (or you may want to do this while under the duvet), such as a roof over your head, running water, your health, your inner strength, your trusted pair of falling-apart trainers, that suit or dress you sold to pay for your kids' school trip, the person who smiled at you in the shop, the box of tissues beside your bed that helps you wipe away your tears…

Will struggled with the concept of gratitude as he saw his 'perfect family world' crumbling. He couldn't see beyond what was going from his life. He said he felt a little stupid for writing down the three things he was grateful for each morning for 21 days (as part of his coaching plan). He said he wrestled with saying thank you and said his DMMs had a field day for the first few days he was doing this. After a while though, Will realised he had so much in his life to be grateful for, including the fact that he was alive and he had healthy children, and although he didn't have what he'd had in his marriage, he now had hopes and dreams for a wonderful future. "Gratitude was a game-changer for me in terms of my mental health, my ability to let go of what I thought I wanted (whether that was the next new toy or gadget, or 'keeping up with the Joneses' – something I hated on so many levels) and to appreciate everything I do have. Life is simpler now, despite having gone through a divorce."

Get into the practice of being grateful for yourself and saying "thank you for showing up" to yourself through your divorce process, every step of the way – because this kindness stuff, while rewarding, takes effort, courage and every ounce of red-knicker/pants ballsiness, and you should never judge your efforts as anything other than personal f*cking brave brilliance.

Try this: Things you can thank yourself for:

- Being you, going through one of the toughest human experiences – no matter how you're coping, you're still here, so thank yourself for that and give yourself a hug

- Not losing your sh*t when your Ex is late, doesn't get back to you with paperwork straight away or says something unkind to you

- Looking after yourself and having a good self-care toolkit in place that you use regularly (put gratitude in there right now!)

- Not talking unkindly about the other parent to your children, no matter how frustrating or anger-inducing your Ex can be

- Choosing a kinder way through the process and being open to doing things differently – this takes courage

Thank your Ex too! I know this may get some of you twitching, but no matter what they've done to you in the past, it's done. You can't change what happened, but you can change how you move on from it. Gratitude is a tool that you can use with your Ex as well as you're working towards having a kinder divorce. This takes daily effort and commitment. With a kinder divorce, you're asked to be vulnerable and open to doing things differently, which is why the practice of gratitude helps. The simple act of saying thank you is an appreciation of everything you or both of you are doing to make this life experience better for you and those you love.

Here are some suggestions (if you need them) of things you can thank your Ex for:

- The good times spent together – dig into those memory banks!
- Still being in your children's lives, no matter how little time is spent – they are still there.
- Showing up to mediation, building solid foundations and committing to building a new future through the process.
- The monthly maintenance and child maintenance payments – I always sent a text saying thank you. It doesn't matter the right or wrong figure of what they are or are not paying, it's still an exchange and the energy behind it is exactly this, so say thank you as you would with anything else in life. (Plus, it's good for the karma bank – just sayin'!)
- The times you felt supported in your work, your accomplishments and when you needed propping up.
- Having the children on the weekends or weeknights that they do. It helps you out, gives you time and your children benefit.

- Helping you learn patience and fortitude, and how to let go and get out of your own way (you can keep this one to yourself rather than thank them directly, if you prefer).
- Creating such beautiful children with you, no matter what happened.

Try this: Write out or say three things each day you're grateful for and three people you have in your life who make a positive difference. Do this every day for 21 days before you go to sleep to help put your brain into a less stressful and more positive state, and grow that appreciation muscle.

"Be thankful that you don't already have everything you desire. If you did, what would there be to look forward to?

Be thankful when you don't know something, for it gives you the opportunity to learn.

Be thankful for the difficult times. During those times you grow.

Be thankful for your limitations, because they give you opportunities for improvement.

Be thankful for your mistakes. They will teach you valuable lessons.

Be thankful when you are tired and weary, because it means you've made a difference.

It's easy to be thankful for the good things.

A life of rich fulfilment comes to those who are also thankful for the setbacks.

Gratitude can turn a negative into a positive.

Find a way to be thankful for your troubles, and they can become your blessings."

Unknown

Gratitude is what got me through my divorce. If you haven't fully integrated gratitude into your life as a divorcee, I suggest it's time to get your gratitude wiggle on and begin.

Health is Wealth

When did you last feel joy in your body? Your body is the best barometer of how stressed you feel. Whatever is going on in your head and the outside world is going to be reflected in your body. If your divorce is not so kind (at the moment), does your body flinch at the monthly lawyer's bill? Or did you feel gut-punched with disappointment at the speeding ticket you got for leaving late for your mediation meeting?

The DMMs are far more likely to behave when your body is nurtured, nourished and noticed (rather than when you're playing catch-up due to a hangover, struggling to focus due to lack of sleep or feeling grumpy as f*ck because you're not eating properly). The DMMs can not only cost you money but also your health, so you need to look out for your health and wellbeing.

Try this: Take a moment to check in with how your body is doing. Is it keeping up with the levels of stress and anxiety in your divorce life? Here's where you start connecting deeply with your body, honouring everything you're putting it through (unintentionally for the most part) and learning how, when you practise self-kindness, your body shows up for you over and over again, supporting your intention to have a kinder divorce.

What do I mean by this?

Our friend cortisol has a hall pass into our body when we experience difficult and challenging life events – like separation and divorce. Cortisol is the stress hormone, and while it helps us stay alert and wary of anything that's likely to attack us, prolonged periods of cortisol can lead to all sorts of problems, such as sleep deprivation, poor diet, addictive habits and making unhelpful decisions.

Try this: Think about how you feel when you haven't eaten for a while, drank enough water or had enough sleep, or when you're feeling under the weather or lonely. What is your go-to – hangry? Irritable or grumpy? Do you get headaches or migraines and then find yourself bedridden with increasing frustration at not being able to do anything well? If you could mitigate these negative emotions, wouldn't divorce life be a little easier, gentler and more peaceful?

The connection between mind and body

Imagine you're worried about seeing your Ex. As you walk towards them, they're standing there looking cross. "Oh no," you think, "what's going to happen now?" Your heart starts pounding, your breath is shallow and you may start to sweat. Your thoughts go wild. Then you look again and they're smiling. It feels better and you're relieved.

If you see your Ex's face looking (what you perceive to be) cross, a whole series of changes might take place in your body. You experience such changes because of what you interpret the reality of this moment to be – in other words, because of the DMMs. When you saw your Ex was actually okay and smiling, a set of calming reactions took place. The way you changed how your body reacted was by noticing that your Ex wasn't actually in a bad mood after all.

How can you change this sort of reaction to one of, as I call it, 'emotionally flatlining' – where you don't fall into the fight, flight or freeze space (the areas where you're most likely to be triggered and where conflict happens, and you're at the mercy of the DMMs)? Imagine what years of high conflict can do to your body if a simple look can induce such heightened emotions?

You change by becoming more skilful at noticing when the DMMs are busily over-catastrophising about what's going to happen when you see your Ex (especially if you have children). Where your thoughts go, your energy goes – so notice when you're thinking too much about what's *going* to happen and be present with what *is*. Take the example of your Ex and the look on their face. It could have been a look as a result of a thought around something they were worried about, or maybe something had happened on the way to the meeting – or it could be they were worrying about seeing you too!

So, how do you connect your health to your life wealth? You get super-good at noticing how you're feeling so you can take a step back from your thoughts and be the observer to what is really happening (rather than what you think is happening). You check in with your body; you take steps to calm your mind using your body, and you begin to take back control of your DMMs rather than them running you. This is why self-care is so important. You're far more likely to be able to manage your thoughts when your body is in good health.

Try this: I've put together a list of suggestions for you to take a look at and integrate into your life. Don't overthink it – check in with your body and notice which suggestions feel helpful and speak to you when you feel a certain way, such as if you're holding your breath, or feeling stress in your gut or back. Each suggestion depends on how much time you have:

- **12 hours:**
    - Get some good quality sleep and integrate self-care – use this as an opportunity to look after yourself.
    - Don't go on a bender and find yourself hungover, playing catch up and feeling ropey.
    - Notice when you're overthinking and practise STOP (S = Stop, T = Take a breath, O = Observe and P = Proceed – refer to the section 'Doing Divorce Differently' in Chapter 2).
    - Try not to gossip or complain about your Ex – you don't need to bring that stuff into your life.
- **2 hours:**
    - Get outside and into nature, or try forest bathing – standing/sitting in a wood and taking deep breaths.
    - Go for a run, swim or do some yoga postures designed to help you feel calm or get all that excess mental energy out of your system.
    - Eat something healthy rather than a sugar-fuelled snack that may get you jittery and feeling all over

the place. If you're a 'hangry' person this suggestion may help you in particular, plus it's self-care – am I sounding like your mother now?

o Don't drink caffeine or sugar-fuelled drinks (even if you haven't been able to sleep) – especially if caffeine or sugar get you punchy with your words and thoughts!

o Meditate before you go to a meeting and get there early – so you go in feeling calmer.

o Rather than scrolling through social media, set a timer for 10 minutes and take some lovely deep breaths, watching your thoughts come and go. (The Divorce Goddess link in the Resources section has free guided meditations you can try.)

o Get organised – for example, if you're travelling, get good at downloading maps, leaving on time, checking the traffic and organising your parking. Playing catch-up is going to set you on edge and your body will feel tense, increasing your stress levels.

- **15 minutes:**

    o If you're nervous, notice where in your body you're feeling your nerves – in your gut, your head or your shoulders? Next, breathe in deeply, imagining you're sending calm to that part of your body through your breath – like you're breathing into that area to calm it.

o Looking hunched up is not a great "I've got it all under control" look. You have two hands, so use them and put them on the sore, tight or stressed area that's making itself known to you; give it a rub as you would a child who's just fallen over, and rub it better. Or you could give yourself a head massage, gently rubbing your head all over with your fingertips. Stretch out, shake your arms and legs, and see with your mind's eye the stress falling down into the ground.

o My favourite practice is Two Steps, One Breath (also covered in Chapter 5 as part of 'The Ninja Toolkit for Children's Wellbeing'). You stand on the ground and push into the ground with your feet, focusing just on your feet. Next, take a deep breath, following the breath with your mind all the way into your belly and back out. Not only does this help 'ground' you (think of an earthing cable to an electrical device) but it also recalibrates your thoughts – especially if they're negative ones going round and round in your head.

o Practise smiling to yourself – put that big cheesy grin on your face and literally sit like this for five minutes (think a mad grin!). Doing this also tells the brain you're feeling happy, and it's also pretty difficult to think negative thoughts while you're smiling – if you don't believe me, try it out for yourself!

o   Go to the bathroom – there's nothing that makes you feel less at ease than feeling uncomfortable because you need the loo!

o   For anyone who wears lipstick – reapply whenever you need to!

And one final tip – if you need courage and strength, and are feeling a little mischievous, then put on some red underwear. Red knickers or boxers aren't just for the bedroom!

Not looking after your body can have you crashing through your divorce on super-charged negative emotions, ready to react rather than respond – and this becomes costly. Many a lawyer's letter has followed a hangover-triggered remark or hangry-based mistake, leading to more conflict.

Applying kindness in your divorce is about your mind, body and spirit. They're all connected, and if you fail to nurture, nourish or notice one part, it can lead to other things not working smoothly (think of a car!). Before you know it, you might see unintended arguments, lateness and unpreparedness wreaking havoc over your efforts to be kind.

Joy is what you do have control over, and it is what you already have in your life. Joy doesn't cherry-pick who has it and who hasn't, and with a few adjustments to your life you can bring even more joy in. Joy is always there, you just have to notice it – even the tiniest glimmer. When you do more accepting and letting go versus holding on and feeling resigned, you're saying yes to your body, mind and soul. This has the ripple effect of you attracting more joy in. Joy is already within you – you just need to give it permission to come out.

Part 3

A Kinder Outcome

When kindness is applied in conflict, it does make a difference. Perhaps not in the way you think or want it to, but it does, in some unexpected way, step in and make its presence known. Call it life magic. It is in those often unnoticed ray-of-sunshine moments, where maybe your Ex's face softens (even a flicker), that a kinder decision or agreement is made. It can be found in the recipe that you both commit to cooking together so you can all eat well, happily and at the same life table, just in separate homes.

In this Part we will begin to explore next steps as you begin to move on and forwards, especially if you have children, and as you get ready to embody and celebrate you.

This book is not to tell you what to do, but is a guide to changing entrenched thought patterns around divorce and how you can feel about your Ex. Yes, there are going to be differences around co-parenting and transiting between new homes and introducing new partners, and maybe just when we think the clouds are parting the next storm clouds will roll in. But as ever, the sky will be blue above them, and although there will be different seasons of thought that test and challenge you as you move into the next stage of the process, you can always find something to be grateful for.

Be open to believing in a life beyond your divorce that is bigger, happier and contains future love, but also understanding that with this life may come dilemmas, trials and tribulations. These may be financial concerns, things your children and teenagers do or do not do, or confidence wobbles, which as we all know are part of being human, divorced or not.

The following chapters are for you to read when you wish, whether when you begin thinking about what your post-divorce life may look like, or when you reach that stage of your life. Always know you are enough; you are figuring things out, as we all are, and I hope the tools I share here will serve you and help you see beyond the storm clouds of conflict, so kindness can rise like the sun does every day.

Chapter 5

The Children Are Alright

Your children really will be alright as you go through divorce or separation; however, the only thing standing in the way of them being okay is whether you, their parents, can see beyond your own misgivings and principled expectations and start the often problematic business of working together to rebuild a future that works for all.

Easier said than done, right? I hear you!

Lebanese poet Kahlil Gibran wrote: "Your children are not your children. They are the sons and daughters of Life's longing for itself. They come through you but not from you, And though they are with you yet they belong not to you." What a wonderful insight.

The thought that my children didn't belong to me but were the sons and daughters of life kind of made sense to me. What I took from this poem was this: as parents we are here to guide, teach and support our children to be who they are as individuals, rather than us 'owning' them. They are their own personalities and are shaped by what we teach, show and share with them.

Our children have their own thoughts around what they see, hear and sense – children's Spidey radars are up there, right?! Manipulating children for our own justification and good or bad future relationship with the other parent is not allowing them to find their own way through the process of what is right or wrong. Hard as it is, children come to their own conclusions at some point in their life, whether in 5, 10, 20 or 40 years. They sense so much and while they may not be emotionally mature enough to articulate their experiences, they will lodge with them for their future, with or without the support of counselling and therapy. As their parent, you always have the choice as to how the experience of separation, divorce and co-parenting 'lands' in all of this, and it depends on whether you can hold fast to kindness for conflict, or not.

This chapter helps you to think beyond your pain and anger, shame and grief – no small ask. I invite you to take your attention away from what has happened with your Ex and to bring your focus back to your children. To choose to show up for yourself in wholeness, authenticity and with kindness, no matter what your Ex does, rather than feeling guilted-out and in conflict. To make what happened better and a life experience for your children to learn from rather than be scarred by, and to create a better life where you can both say in years to come, "We did our best for our children with the experience, tools and knowledge we had at the time."

Remember, your children are not going to be children forever. You have only a finite amount of time with them: be gracious, make their childhood and teenage years work for them, and remember kindness by observing and responding rather than reacting and pulling the kindness plug on all the good work.

This chapter also reminds you to be gentle on yourself if you've made mistakes – remember, you don't have a blueprint for this. It can be heartbreaking to see your children in the middle of your Ex's messed up, angry divorce process, especially if they haven't committed to kindness in conflict. Sometimes you have no choice but to hold your counsel or else possibly end up being separated from your children by the insidious practice of parental alienation (which is the practice of one parent turning their children against the other parent). Consider this: if divorce is teaching your children valuable life skills and you can support them to understand your separation without anger, but with patience towards your Ex, then there is some good coming out of all this. Our lives are all about possibilities (see the section 'Opportunities and Possibilities' in Chapter 6 for more on this); not always immediate possibilities that happen 'now', but ones that, when they happen, remind us of the good work that we've done in the past. For instance, this book would never have been written without my own experiences of divorce as a child, and then as an adult.

In this chapter, we'll consider:

- Managing the shift from one home to two places your children may call home
- Achieving happier handovers
- Using some helpful tools to support your children through the divorce process
- Making holidays work for everyone – especially the children
- Starting new relationships when children are involved
- Navigating family events with minimal drama

Two Homes

Home is indeed where the heart is, and that's no different for your children, even if they will now have two homes. Two homes can be simply two places filled with love and kindness, with a feeling of safety; somewhere for your children to be nourished and held by one of their parents on those difficult and sad days.

However, if you're finding it hard getting used to your children having two homes – with the endless travelling, negotiating, reasoning, adjusting and the newness of it all – just think for a moment how your children may be feeling.

It's not easy for any of you. Period. Applying kindness, especially when you find yourself in a difficult place around who and what are where, is not an easy way forward, but it's definitely the least painful and conflictual. To know that kindness was at the centre of every decision, conversation and action that you, your Ex or both of you took to secure the sanctity of your children's childhood through and beyond your divorce is the difference to your children's future (and yours) moving forward.

"You run a loose ship," said a client's Ex one day while talking about the rules around their teenagers. Fortunately, this worked, with each equally happy to be good cop and bad cop, with a middle ground where everyone agreed to be honest: there was no playing off one against the other (including the teenagers), and in the end neither of them ended up being the strict parent. The teenagers were happy they didn't have to hide from either parent – it was all out there and everyone was happy.

Kinder co-parenting and managing two homes is an easier way forward than being married to someone who doesn't approve very much of your parenting skills. If you're both signed up to the fact that you run your homes differently and appreciate what the other brings to the table in terms of parenting, what happens where and why, then you have half a chance of making this work. Let go of the divorce mind monkeys (DMMs) trying to create strife and being competitive.

Ground rules, however, are a must that you both need to get on the table so the children know there's no wriggle room to play you off against each other. The following is a guide to reducing conflict so you're all garnering the benefits of what two homes brings to a divorced family, rather than being hampered by this change.

Note: 'Nesting' is a way for families who are going through separation and divorce to still use the family home as the location for when either parent has their time with their children. There is usually a smaller place rented for the other parent, perhaps until the family house is sold.

Visiting hours

For many couples (especially those who have agreed to be kinder to each other), there's a tendency in the beginning to keep visiting hours more flexible with no firm boundaries or times to call. If you are in this space, you could both agree to do a family supper one night a week or at the weekend, easing you all into your different life together and making it gentler for your children.

If your Ex wants to come round to see the children, make it a firm but flexible arrangement for the first few months so you can experience what works for you all, until it is legally agreed. Write this in your Intention so it's not misconstrued and your Ex has this to hand. Be as clear as you can, with kindness, so everyone knows where they stand. If you not being in your house makes it easier for all during your Ex's visit, then go and see a friend or go to the gym; use this time wisely to do something for you.

There's no blueprint for what is right, and learning to have a kinder, less conflictual divorce is having the courage to communicate honestly, truthfully and bravely. Flexibility is something else I would urge you both to consider – agree what is okay and what isn't; boundaries again. But be ever mindful of the DMMs lurking, ready to seize an opportunity to create unnecessary strife between you both. Keep your children as your focus, make it about them not you and remember: sometimes you have to be a bigger person for an easier life. Remembering kindness is clever. If you want to take time to get really clear, then I suggest you both write out your needs, desires and expectations around seeing the children in the early days and/or managing two homes and try to find the important and necessary middle ground – always with your children in mind.

Try this: Here are some areas you might want to consider:

- If one of you is ill, are you able to pop over to help out by taking round a meal or adjusting the childcare (and collect some brownie points, especially if your weekend off is coming up)?

- If a child feels wobbly about staying with the other parent, what is the plan? Do you stay until they're settled, do you go, or do they come back with you? How are you both going to manage this? Make this part of your plan to prevent later conflict!

- Include your older children/teenagers so they feel they are part of the process by asking them for suggestions that work for them so you both know and can then manage your own emotions such as fear, rejection and sadness better if they arise (especially if they want to hang out with their friends).

- Have an agreed plan, but also be flexible if you're doing one week on/one week off. If the children have great news to share with the other parent, allow this to happen in person or online; work with the children's lives and their wins.

- If one of you has a new partner, decide on the protocols of meeting them (see the section 'Introducing New Partners', later in this chapter, for more). Make it about your children first: teach them that you, as adults, can do this and do it well (mostly)!

Kindness for conflict is also about minimising the conflict within children through divorce. Children very often have divided loyalties – they love both parents and have thoughts and feelings they may want to share, but they may feel conflicted and feel unable to share. Many children love the chance to be heard as it makes them feel important and included. Something you may want to explore if you find sitting down and talking together difficult is child-inclusive mediation. This is something you may want to bring up with your mediator if they haven't already mentioned it.

I was due to go on holiday with my new partner and my Ex was coming to pick up the children for the week. As he turned up, an old boyfriend and his son also turned up for a cuppa. So, I finished packing and left the guys to chat. Was it easy? They were a little unsure, but I settled my DMMs and went with the flow as an easier way forward because the unexpected does happen. With the best-laid plans there's always room for things to go awry, so again there's a choice: be chill or kick off. That afternoon we all went with the flow. It didn't need to be anything more than a bunch of adults having a cuppa and a chat in the sunshine; rare, I grant you, but we never know when those kinder foundations are going to be relied upon for future easier and happier days. The children saw it too, and by removing the DMMs from messing with a situation that was totally unexpected but okay, it made me realise the groundwork on kindness prepared us for an experience like this.

Different spaces

So, beginning with the cosy and known versus new and unfamiliar. You split up the worldly chattels into two homes, or maybe the old home stays fully furnished and the new home is then furnished from new (or old – charity shops, auctions and junk shops are full of great pieces that have been preloved, which are more interesting and greater if you're looking to save money). If you can agree, try to incorporate old with the new so your children have a sense of the familiar even in the new place, with the much-loved cosy armchair; family photos and pictures; a favourite cup. Getting territorial (other than with family heirlooms) can be detrimental to your children being able to transition better between the two houses and can lead to resistance for them to visit. This ultimately impacts your time off too, so choose the less conflictual route and let go. Children also have an innate sense of fairness, so bear this in mind too with the division of your chattels.

As a child of divorced parents, Andrew can remember the weekends in his dad's new place. While sometimes it stung when he saw reminders of family days together, it was still good to see the familiar – like an old duvet set in his dad's house, particularly as it had been replaced by a newer, less liked set at his mum's!

You may want to ask your children what they would prefer or ask them to write what they would like in their two new homes. After all, it is your children who are travelling between the two and not you! Communication for two happier homes is key.

Each parent to their own

Please try to resist criticising your Ex over how they choose to live in their own home. Obviously, with the children over, the basics like cleaning, tidying and fresh sheets would be lovely, as well as having laundry detergent available to have your children's school uniform ready for Monday morning. I can't tell you the frustration of the other parent when they find out the laundry hasn't been done over the weekend, and a late-night washing and drying session has to happen on Sunday night! This is stuff you can avoid and you have control over. Making an effort to have your home nice and tidy not only helps you prepare on all levels for your children, but as a child of divorced parents it is enough to come into a different space, so make it one that is prepared with love for them. Forgive yourself if you don't do it for a week, but observe how much more stressful it gets when you're not organised. If you're finding it difficult to keep it all together, you might want to ask for help. There is no failure in not holding it together during the first months of separation, but there is failure in not asking for support. Check in with each other – what do you both need to make this work? Don't be tempted to use this as weaponry at a later stage.

Kindness is the path between two homes: keep it safe, respectful and tidy of unkind thoughts, words and actions

Bear in mind that divorce means two different ways of parenting, house rules and attitudes.

If you're feeling annoyed by how your Ex is doing their thing with the children, consider:

- There's a reason why you're getting divorced, and maybe those habits that irritated you before are now the ones you can let go of (if they're not harming the children).
- Let the children see there are different ways of doing things in life – it's an opportunity for them to experience and understand more about how life really works with different personalities involved.
- You don't have to like how your Ex approaches parenting, but if your Ex loves the children and they're happy, why should this be an issue? Obviously, any ground rules around bedtimes, screen time, pocket money and any of the usual parental bugbears need to be agreed upon so you

and your Ex are coming from a mutual set of agreed intentions. This may be a co-parenting plan or intention document you both may wish to create so you are both coming from the same place to reduce conflict. You get to do it your way in your home, being happy and confident that the home you create is one filled with love and feels safe.

- The key role of kindness in all of this is the ability for you to let go, resist the need to control (nod to the DMMs), and accept and welcome differences! If your children are safe, happy and loved by your Ex – so what if your parenting styles are wildly different?! If your Ex can afford bigger and better things than you can, that's okay, it doesn't make you a failure or any less of a parent. Always remember you are your child's parent too, and whatever you serve up at their table, if done with love and kindness, will be what they'll remember, always.

Happier Handovers

Co-parenting is the act of two parents raising their child/children together, even though they're no longer romantically involved. Ideally, both parents work with each other to ensure their children have a safe and loving environment to grow up in, and with a commitment to keep communication respectful, open and kind.

Co-parenting is mostly about pick-ups, drop-offs and the important conversations in between. Remember... the toing and froing of children in divorced life is what they, not you, have to go through. Each week the children are the ones going back and forth, sitting in the car, packing/repacking while we have time out... It is them moving, not us, especially after a hard week at school where they might just want to hang out in one place and maybe see their friends. Even if we have to make a two-hour Friday night drive, we need to get over ourselves and work to make this happen for them. Bringing your children into focus is key to happier handovers. As parents, we need to be on board, kind and sorted... it's the least we can do.

One of the biggest stressors for children is not knowing what is happening and when. Not everyone is an organisational whizz, so for the children's sake, especially in the initial months, try to help your Ex get sorted by supporting them with helpful (not condescending) suggestions that come from a place of patience and kindness. Let go of the frustrations you had when you were married; encourage rather than discourage. Believe me and many of my clients – this pays dividends.

Try this: Here are some ideas for you to open up to a kinder approach and reduce conflict:

- Be flexible with your thoughts by noticing your resistance to supporting (in the smallest ways) your Ex – override the DMMs, especially if you know this will make your life easier!

- Perhaps gift your Ex (with kindness) a children's visit diary or set up an electronic diary or app (see the Resources section for examples of co-parenting apps).

- Handing over at the same location works by keeping everyone knowing what's what. Make it as halfway as possible and easy for you both to get to, especially on Friday or Sunday nights. If you are close enough to walk the children round, then great (don't drop them off further down the street to avoid seeing your Ex as one parent told me – this isn't a walk of shame for the children!).

- Pre-plan timing. Weekends don't always happen exactly as we want them to, especially if there are birthday parties or family gatherings. Do deals with each other and bank brownie points. Learn to work with each other and, above all, try to be flexible. If one of you is taking liberties, you know kindness is on the line, so try to be reasonable.

- Have an action plan if you're running late – speak to each other so you know what's going on. I knew a couple who had pieces of fruit attributed to time frames so they didn't get into the details or an argument, they simply texted – for example, a pineapple was 10 minutes. Have the respect and courage to be honest: if you're always running late, consider – is this kindness?

- What is the cancellation process if either of you are unwell, have a sick parent or car troubles? Plan in advance how you both will manage with kindness.

- Resist the need to know everything, questioning the children as soon as they arrive home or get in the car. Let them have their decompression time and settle back into your home, especially if they're tired and don't want to talk. Try not to automatically assume something is wrong. Let them tell you when they're ready, and if you have a kind co-parenting relationship, one not fraught with outbursts and sly comments, the children will feel more comfortable and confident to share any thoughts or worries. Good co-parenting gives them this space to do so.

- Support your children to feel happier about seeing their other parent: take favourite toys; snuggle blankets; school uniform; swim gear and have it all packed, ready to go. Children worry a lot about forgotten stuff so help them pack, encourage them and lovingly support them. If they're older, give them a list of what to remember to bring back – they are learning valuable life skills in getting themselves organised (especially if your Ex is still not on top of this stuff). When children are organised, they're far less likely to kick off and resist moving from home to home as it helps decrease their feelings of stress and anxiety (and yours).

- Do a regular review of what is at each parent's house and what isn't. Rebalance by having spare clothes/kit/toys/toiletries to save on future difficulties. If you can afford it, double up on essentials so there are no worries about the bits forgotten.

You can't organise your Ex

Aaaahhhh, the frustrations and the lack of control over your Ex – if there are any micro-managing DMMs lurking, weed them out! Yes Exes can be difficult, and even more so when you're no longer together. They can be tempted to use your children as a weapon by being deliberately late or unaccommodating. Sadly, this is not only unhelpful, but comes from victimhood rather than an empowered place.

Hopefully the following observations will encourage you to be a bigger person, to think more about what is happening around pick-ups/drop-offs and to make this part of your divorce work for those you love most (also, reread the 'Acceptance Versus Holding On' section in Chapter 4).

Try this: Part of a kinder divorce is also appreciating and understanding that we are all human. Sometimes we stumble and we don't always get it right... so:

- Remember, Exes have bad days too; they might not be sleeping well, they may be feeling ill, they may be feeling angry, sad, guilty... you can't change this. Choose your battles. Write some boundary rules together that you can stick in your Divorce Intention (or create a separate Co-Parenting Intention) and practise letting the small stuff go.

- Handovers are not about you or your Ex, they are about your children. Kindness, respect and understanding for your own peace of mind, and for your children, is what you do have control over – by simply taking a deep breath and letting the inner control freakery take a holiday. You may want to do this by adopting a practice like taking a deep breath when you notice a difficult thought, or doing the Two Step, One Breath activity in the later 'The Ninja Toolkit for Children's Wellbeing' section in this chapter.

- For repeat offenders on lateness, disorganisation and disrespecting each other's time, and making the children bear the brunt of such actions, give them this book, help them get organised or let it go. Forcing someone to do something they can't or don't want to do is like giving them your Velcro so they can stick more conflict to it each time. If you are the 'late' person, know this: you could just be ramping up the conflict and inadvertently adding to the stress felt by your children.

Remember, you can organise yourself. Begin with you first, and get yourself in order. When you are in order, you'll find it easier to manage (emotionally and mentally) an Ex who chooses not to be.

Try this: Here are a few tried and tested ways for you to manage divorce stress, anxiety and worries:

- Check in with your own stress barometer as to how you're feeling before pick-up or drop-off. What do you need to do to help you feel better? Make checking in with yourself a priority before you see your Ex.

- Find your calm mojo before the handover: meditate, breathe deeply, go for a walk, be cool and remember to accept and let go of what your Ex thinks. Prove them wrong and get organised: you owe it to yourself and it's good self-care!

- Don't be tempted to drink coffee, alcohol or sugary drinks before pick-up or drop-off – basically, anything that's going to ramp up the anxiety and make you feel 'angsty'. If you're managing a hangover and likely to be grumpy, mitigate massively by drinking lots of water, eating something healthy and recognising the signs that you could be easier to trigger.

- Try not to fuel your thoughts and fears about your Ex with a bitchin' session beforehand with a friend or family member. If there's stuff that needs talking about, make an appointment with your Ex; write an email (and sit on it overnight before sending) to do this, rather than organising it at a pick-up/drop-off.

Try this: There is always something you can do to make handovers kinder. See which of these ideas work for you and use them!

- List four small self-care things that you can do pre- or post-pick-up/drop-off to help you show up for yourself and be proud that you did it. Book an alarm on your phone beforehand so you actually do them!
- Try to be smiley with your Ex – smiling helps us feel better! Not a comedic, grit-your-teeth, frozen-face smile, but a genuine, warm and soft smile. Practise in the car on the way there!
- Truly wish your gorgeous children a wonderful weekend with their dad/mum; gift them your genuine, beautiful smile so they can relax, knowing that it will be fine and you'll be okay without them.

- Don't be tempted to do a 'poor me' act to your Ex (or children) to induce guilt, hard as it feels if you've nothing planned for the weekend. This is handing away your power and energy and keeps you in victim mode, so it's a no to that! Change it up so you don't have to feel this way; plan stuff and get out there – you can do this! (Plus, you don't want your children worrying about you while they're away.)

- Check in and acknowledge how much better you feel when these times are more gentle, kind and compassionate. Where do you feel it in your body? Were you left feeling relaxed and relieved – is this better than stressed with a stomach all knotted up? Even if your Ex is not so signed up, know that you've been kind and that's enough.

- Is being a bigger person with your Ex in front of your children really that hard? How good would it feel now and in the future for your children not to stress about you both? After all, your divorce is not their fault!

The Ninja Toolkit for Children's Wellbeing

I am passionate about children's wellbeing throughout divorce. It is incumbent on us as parents to get our shizzle in order so we can be there for those who need us to be in a good place! But equally important is to empower our children with practices that they can take with them into their future life. In this section, I've put together a few of the most popular tools from my time teaching mindfulness in schools that I hope will appeal to your children too. You can also get in on this by trying some of these together so you all benefit. Remember, children learn by example (although it may not always feel like it) – they do listen and helpful stuff does land!

I cannot tell you the power of creating a space in your life to talk about emotions and worries and to just get it out there in a form that children relate to! Divorce is a huge opportunity for you all to learn so much and apply kindness to yourselves as you build those future foundations with your children.

The saying goes that we are only as happy as our unhappiest child, and this Ninja Toolkit is full of ideas to help your children when they're feeling wobbly about what is happening to you as a family, if they feel wobbly at your Ex's house, or if they're experiencing strife with friends or school that is heightened by what's happening at home.

These are in no particular order and all worthy of a try!

A Worry Box

Find a special box or handmade school pot that you've collected along the way. Ours was a clay painted turtle pot with a lid, one we couldn't throw away – because one day it was to have the best use we could have hoped for: to help us through the hard days.

In the early days of separation, my children (then aged 7 and 9) were sometimes a bit out of sorts (understandably so), with this life change taking its toll. We don't have a blueprint on dealing with unexpected emotions that arise unannounced, and I realised we needed to talk, to get creative about talking and make it fun!

Enter the Worry Box! If they had a worry, they would write it down and put it in the turtle. After supper (less hangry), we would stay at the table (a good excuse to eat together) and check the turtle. We'd take turns to read the worries in there, such as tricky friends at school, mummy and daddy being okay, what was going to happen, missing the other parent, exams. Include yours too if they are appropriate to share with your children without worrying them even more. For example, if you worry that you're not sleeping properly and feeling grumpy, you have the opportunity to talk about how to get more sleep. After the worry was read out, we'd take turns to suggest ways to help make the worry better. It was bonding and kind, and everyone felt heard and supported. Many worries came up and were addressed that may have been buried or ruminated on.

Belly Breathing

This is a simple way for your children to settle any butterflies caused by anxiety or worries. Belly breathing happens naturally when they're babies, and breathing into their bellies triggers their body's natural relaxation response. It's a gentle way to settle thoughts and can also settle them to be able to sleep, or get back to sleep:

- Get your child to lie down on their back, or sit down putting their hands on their belly, which feels comforting.
- Tell them to take a deep breath in and out through their nose, following the air down into their belly. They might want to imagine they are inflating a balloon in their belly with the in-breath, and deflating it on the out-breath; or they can place a small toy on their belly when they are lying down and watch it go up and down with their breath.
- Do this several times and if they notice the worry coming back, get them to go back to following their breath in and out.
- Ask if this helped them; if it did, encourage them to use this in future (and share the practice with their friends).

HAILT

Sometimes we don't want to talk but really need people to understand how we're feeling, right? So write out this list for your fridge door, children's bedroom and your Ex's place as a check-in if you or the children are feeling worried or anxious. Instead of a mega deep-and-meaningful chat that feels difficult, your child can simply point to the word that describes how they're feeling so everybody gets it, understands better and can then take actions to remedy the feeling.

H	–	Hungry
A	–	Angry
I	–	Ill
L	–	Lonely
T	–	Tired

Katherine used this with her youngest, Sam, who was 7 years old. "He didn't want to speak, he missed his dad terribly and it was awful to see him bottling it all up and then exploding with frustration. My Ex and I introduced HAILT to both households at the same time and it worked. When the children knew they could share how they were feeling in both homes, it was a game-changer. All it took was a 'How do you feel?' and we all knew then how to manage how Sam was feeling. If he was lonely and missing his dad, he'd video-call him and all would be well. I knew I couldn't be everything to my children – I didn't want to be – and to do this I needed to learn to be open and sensitive to their needs."

HAILT can open up conversations more easily, and children (and you) get to practise self-kindness – it feels better when we share. Were they hungry because they hadn't eaten lunch at school due to worries? This tool helps children to talk about their emotions, how they're feeling and how they can help themselves – if they're both angry and hungry, hangry means eat!

Happy List

You might want to encourage your children to create a Happy List, something I've shared in schools. It's a list of things they can do to help them feel happier and less anxious. It can include things like playing outside, playing music or dancing, getting creative by writing, painting or drawing, having a nap or a cuddle, or calling their other parent if they're missing them.

Ask your children to design their own Happy List and put it up in their bedroom as an empowering reminder to manage how they're feeling through tricky times.

Two Steps, One Breath

This is a great tool for stopping the train of worrying thoughts. Ask your child to think of a worry. Ask them who's in the worry, what's happening in the worry, where do they feel it in their body? Then, ask your child to walk around with this worry in their head until you say "stop". On "stop", your child pushes their feet into the ground, or stamps if they prefer, and takes a deep breath, following their breath down into their belly and back out. With each of these actions, encourage your child to focus on their feet and their breath. Ask them to notice afterwards if the worry is still as strong. If not, that's great! Practise more! They can use this at school before a test, a goal kick or going on stage, or if they're anxious about pick-ups/drop-offs.

Hopefully, these ninja practices will resonate with you and your children, to support them more through this time and help them learn to help themselves.

Holidays

Holidays, especially the first ones for all of you after separation, may be the most painful. These can be times when vulnerability, grief and the reality of the loss of the traditional family unit are felt most keenly. The old ways don't work and yet there's no current blueprint for how holidays are going to work in the future. Beliefs, values and money can all create conflict around holidays. However, try to flip your thoughts to see this as an opportunity to have that holiday you've always been hankering after!

Mark said, "Holidays went from a chore and arguments over whose turn it was to look after the children and obligatory 'holiday' sex, to each of us spending really good quality time with our children as single parents. We each had the holidays we wanted, did the things we most loved, shared them with our children, bonded more and, importantly, had fun."

As with everything in this process, communication is key. If you think that a camping trip with your mates and kids somewhere remote is your ideal summer holiday, consider if this is really going to work for your teenagers or children. It might appeal, it might not, so be prepared for negotiating with your children or changing your plans. Bear in mind too that they may talk with your Ex about this, so be prepared for how you're going to feel if your Ex tries to convince you to do something else...

You might want to plan a trip each so you can both get an idea of what the children are going to experience, whether they'll be okay away from the other parent and whether you can afford the holiday you want to take. Write 'be flexible' in large letters on the top of the planning page and remember, this is your opportunity to make holidays good and memorable in the future. (And don't forget, you get time off from parenting duties while the children are away!)

Katie took her children on holiday and while out in restaurants she felt tears prickle at families giving them what she thought was the "sad face of divorce" look. Until she realised that none of them were talking to each other and she wondered if there may be a hint of jealousy at the fun and laughter going on at her own table. We never know what is going on in other people's lives...

Try this: To reduce possible conflict and to avoid DMM thoughts of a competitive nature, here are some thoughts around managing holidays:

- Email each other PROPOSED dates or use a calendar/co-parenting app (see the Resources section for some good examples) and see which dates work, then move forwards from there.

- Put a budget together – especially if funds will be the game-changer. If you're out to punish your Ex with a big expensive holiday because you believe they owe you (even if they do), ask yourself – is this feeding the narrative of punishing them and spending money that might be better allocated at a later date? Actions resulting from anger rarely result in good memories and bulk up more emotional baggage (and debt) to clear later.

- Make the holidays about the children; this keeps you both out of the conflict zone of selfishness. Kindness reigns, the sun shines and holidays with your children aren't going to be forever, right? Enjoy these precious moments together while they last.

- If things are tricky, remember to get permission from your Ex to take your children abroad – and if jumping ship is going to cause ructions when you return, ask yourself: is it worth it? Sometimes trying something closer to home to keep the peace is easier and less hot in more ways than one!

A friend was due to take her children abroad for a family wedding until her Ex went to court to stop them. In all of this sadness she thought, "F*ck it, I'm going back on the dating apps," and her first date was the man she fell in love with, and they're still together. Sometimes things happen for a reason and we just never know why at the time. To this day she silently thanks her Ex for the day he made that call to his lawyer.

If you feel nervous about holidaying on your own with your children, remember:

- Put yourself right out of your comfort zone and just do it – there are many single parents out there all doing it too!
- You never know what's going to happen until you try – who you're going to meet, make new friends with and share the good, bad and ugly with!
- You get to celebrate the fact that you're not 'getting through' the annual holiday, with nothing much to talk about, resentment flowing from dawn to dusk and crap holiday sex that kinda keeps everything going until next year.

- The kids get the gift of two holidays, one with each parent – how brilliant is that? It's an upgraded summer!
- If you're finding the prospect too difficult, ask your parents or siblings to come along and help – people love being asked and with most grandparents wanting to feel useful during this time, make the most of any offers too.

There's nothing like spending time in a new place with your children. I took my two teenagers to Rome for my 50th birthday and they sang happy birthday to me in the Piazza Navona on a Sunday afternoon with a huge gelato and lit a candle to blow out by the fountains. We will never forget it, nor the time I left my driving licence in the UK and we had to bus it for five hours across a Greek island in August heat with heavy suitcases. (We'll leave that one there!!) This is what making memories – good and bad – is all about!

If you miss your holidays with your Ex, hold those memories close as a wonderful gift, and see now as an opportunity to make new ones.

You now have the option to holiday on your own – a guilt-free holiday without children – with friends, a lover, strangers or on your own (head to the 'Changing FOMO to JOMO (the Glorious Joy of Missing Out)' section in Chapter 3 for some ideas!).

Christmas and Religious Festivals

These events can be dreaded times of year, irrespective of divorce and the extra stress that comes with dividing a family into two. I invite you to remember that Christmas is just one day, and when making plans aim to hold the thoughts of equal time and flexibility with each parent in mind. You don't have your children forever and for the first Christmas post-separation, think selflessly. Tough, but trust you will get (albeit painfully) through it and you will survive; you'll never have another first Christmas, religious festival or holiday once the challenging first one is out of the way. Remember: you can do hard things and you can do this – it's not forever! See this time as an opportunity to make new traditions that are just for you and the children – that you can share whenever they ARE with you.

Try this: It is never going to be easy, whether it is your first time or not, so pull your brave pants (or festive jumper) on with these suggestions:

- If this is the first Christmas/religious holiday, try to do this time together, for your children. Let them see you both committed to them with kindness to each other. (Grimace in private if you need to!)

- Decide on a plan and stick to it. If you're apart, be respectful by giving equal time to each other and arranging other stuff around that plan.

- If others are planning to host or join you, let them know as soon as you can so they can plan ahead with less stress.

- Tell your children what the plan is so they know what is happening and can get excited!

- Resist putting your own traditional celebratory 'lens' on what the children will think during this time – if you're okay, they'll be okay!

- Each write down the areas you think will trigger you and share them so you're both aware (be mindful and remove emotional words, or ask a friend to read it beforehand).

- Be mindful of alcohol consumption – it's emotional topping up.

- Do buy each other a (nice) gift, maybe get the children to help choose it.

- Share the chores on the day if together (well done by the way – it's tough!). Remember you're on the path of doing it differently, so if you didn't help out before then try this time so there's no room for resentment and conflict.

- Know you can always take time out to breathe deeply in the bathroom or take the dog (or yourself) for a walk – you have choices, remember! Time out is essential whether you are getting on well or not. Don't wait until conflict lands.

- If there are family Zoom calls on the day and you're invited to participate and it feels okay, wish your Ex's family happy Christmas/festival/holidays. Your children will see this – brownie points/bigger person opportunity here!

- It is about your children.

I remember the first Christmas and the associated money concerns. The children had stockings and four presents each: one to wear, one to read, one to play with and something useful. Surprisingly they loved this, which removed the competitive multiple purchasing element.

Birthdays

The same rules apply here as for Christmas and religious holidays (refer to the preceding section), but consider these points too:

- If your Ex is 'birthday forgetful', instead of slating them, remind them for your children's sake – yes it's a pain, but it's important.

- Buy a card/present for your Ex from the children – do not let them feel the stress of forgetting.

- Be helpful at parties; if you cook, offer to make the cake and don't be late!

- Resist imbibing alcohol at your children's parties!

- If you can't make a birthday event, arrange a call online. Book it in so your Ex isn't wondering what you're going to do – which would otherwise be fertile ground for the DMMs and conflict.

Introducing New Partners

Meeting a new partner can be a double-edged sword; the excitement of possible new love and a relationship are now extensively coupled with not just yours, but others' feelings in there too. I read a great article about a couple who both had three children each, who when they got together worked out that they were not just balancing each other's emotions, but also those of their six children, their Exes, their Exes' new partners, their parents-in-law, sisters- and brothers-in-law, cousins, friends... It was enormous, but their relationship worked! This story stayed with me; thoughts of you and your new beau are only just the beginning!

If your Ex meets someone new before you have split, this is going to be anger-inducing, painful and difficult – use your own words here (write out how you feel). This is fertile ground for creating a neural pathway of hate that is going to be harder to get out of, especially if you're fuelled by vengeful social media posts and friends' experiences. The DMMs love this and while I know you feel wronged, I urge you to be mindful of creating negative neural pathways of hate, which are going to take time to heal (I hear you, by the way).

However, this is about the children, not you… it's crap, I know, but try to keep your children the focus in all of this. If this rankles, flicks your ear and makes you mad, then know this: you are not in the position of going anywhere near the new partner just yet. Accept the relationship; don't say "Never will I ever meet that *****", and please start doing the work (coaching/therapy/ counselling) to get you through this. This is the difference between a happier future and a frankly sh*t one for your children, for you and everyone around you all. If you were left for this other person, it is incumbent on you to try to be a bigger person (I hear you, and if you've just thrown this book on the floor, please do pick it up again!). Think of it this way – the bigger you are, the higher you rise in the karmic stakes (for starters). Good things will come to you! Own this part of the healing process and grow your inner strength!

Dealing with your Ex's new partner presents you with a most powerful choice. Believe you can do this one thing for yourself. Show your Ex and their new partner that you really are the coolest frickin' Ex that ever walked the earth – and, seriously, would they be expecting that?! Believe me and all the other clients who've resisted their DMMs wanting to scream blue murder at the new party and who didn't, and now live a simpler, easier and less angry life.

So let's get you on the path towards introducing your new partner to your children.

Your new partner

Firstly, don't rush, especially if yours or your Ex's new relationship played a role in ending the marriage. Children need time to accept that their parents' relationship is over. If new partners are introduced too soon, children may feel they are being replaced, no matter how much you tell them otherwise. Be patient.

If you can be open by letting your children know you're feeling ready for someone to come into your life, this can help prepare them, especially if you've started dating. For some children this may come as a relief that their mum or dad isn't going to end up on their own. This can be both exciting and scary – so start slowly and get a feel for what's going to work for your children and what isn't.

I know, I know, you've found love again and you want to tell the world! Resist the temptation to be 'social media loved up' (especially if your Ex is still unhappy). (Chapter 2 considers the challenging subject of social media in 'Walking the Talk: Social Media Murder and Pain Hunting'.) Be patient; your children need time to get to know your new partner, plus your new partner may also need help with knowing what to expect from your children, especially if they don't have children of their own – so many variables!

Let your children know they're still your priority. This is a very different and sometimes scary time for them to accept and they may now be resistant, despite earlier excitement. Ask them about their worries, listen to them and reassure them. Depending on what sort of day or week they've had, the last thing they may want to accept is your new partner. Be open and flexible and do 'deals' with them so they feel they are being heard and have some control, so they're less likely to kick up so much as a result. For example, maybe offer more screen time, a sleepover or extra ice cream, or agree to a family check-in regularly to see how they're feeling.

Meeting the children
Plan your new partner's meeting with your children; be kind so it can pay off in the future. You have the opportunity now to make powerful choices that can alleviate future stress, anxiety and conflict.

Try this: Here are some suggestions so it can work for you all:

- Choose a neutral location and a fun activity so they get to see what your new partner is about.

- Don't try to fit it in at the end of a busy weekend – this stuff is important. It can be the make or break, so don't rush!

- Think about how you're going to introduce your children to your new partner – check in with your kids to find out what they would like the person to know about them, and what they want to know about your partner. You might want to think of things that your children and new partner have in common – pets, sport, music, films – let both sides know so there is some commonality and similar expectations.

- Try not to tell your kids "You'll really like so-and-so" – what if they don't? What then? Children may think there's something wrong with them for not liking your new partner. Keep the meeting free of expectations. "I know you're going to get along really well" – if that's not pressure, I don't know what is!

- If you're meeting your new partner's children, I can tell you from experience that being warm, being friendly and being you is the best. Authenticity is what we all love, and this includes children. Also, finding that middle ground between being friendly and not too over-the-top is key – so just be you!

- When both partner's children meet, it's a big thing for everyone – this could be the make or break, hard rather than easy, so perhaps ease them in gently with brunch or a cup of hot chocolate first. Maybe share what the other children like so they find commonality, as forcing something may block the flow – and the more the parents relax, the more the children will. So try not to stress and do your self-care first, trusting the children hopefully will find their way to friendship if the parents get out of the way!

Once you've got some ideas on the points above, you may wish to share them with your new partner and older children to help everyone involved know what to expect. Try to notice when you're trying too hard – children sense it, so remember their Spidey radars. Teenagers may be easier; they have their own stuff going on in their hormonal heads, anyway!

Your Ex's new partner

We aren't conditioned to like our Ex's new partner, but how about you let this go for the sake of your children. This is a great opportunity to show your Ex and their new partner just how cool you really are.

It's not going to be easy knowing your Ex is introducing their new partner to your children while you're on a child-free weekend. Despite the DMMs doing their dementor thing in your head, perhaps increasing your feelings of loneliness and failure, anger and shame, it's important to please try and approach things in as positive a light as you possibly can. At the very least, think emotional flatlining, water off a duck's back… and don't forget you have a choice, so go straighten your crown!

Let your children make up their own minds about the new partner, without influencing them.

Try this: However you're feeling about your Ex being with someone else and meeting your children, come back to self-care as events like this are where the DMMs get sneaky and blindside you with unexpected emotions:

- Plan to do something lovely with a friend over the time of the meeting.
- Resist the temptation to check with any of your children on how things are going. (Although if your children are upset while they're away, agree to have an online call. They maybe also want to check on you, too – it's a big thing for children meeting a potential 'new parent'.)
- Your children may be fearful of telling you they had a lovely time, so please try not to interrogate!
- Try to focus on the children's positive experience and whether they enjoyed themselves, rather than the negative.

- Take a deep breath, notice the pitch of your voice (if it's stressed, the children will know) and with every bit of your strength and amazingness let your children know it's okay for them to talk about their other parent's new partner (but again, don't interrogate them!).

- Encourage your children to talk to you if they have any worries, concerns and other feelings around meeting or being with the new partner. Please do be supportive rather than judgey and pass any helpful feedback to your Ex so they can make any adjustments to smooth things moving forwards. Don't poke the bear with this one, no matter how tempting – this is for your children, not you.

If you need time to come to terms with the new relationship, then perhaps get yourself focused on something completely different – start training for a marathon or start writing a book! If you need to, scream a lot in the car on your own rather than let it all out in front of your children.

Try this: Take some time to write a few sentences down about:

- How you feel about your Ex's relationship with their new partner.

- Specifically, your Ex's new partner (if you've already met them).

Look at your words and ask yourself: can I flip them so they are better for everyone – including myself? For example, do they make your Ex happy (so the heat is off you)? Are they a good person? Do you trust them with your children? Try to remember that at one time your Ex was (hopefully) a good person for you and so they have the potential to choose a good and kind future partner. This is why working on forgiveness is so powerful, especially when children are involved. They are more likely to relax and be happy at your Ex's and with their new partner (allowing you weekends off) if you are okay, so try and resist spewing anger at the new partner. Client experiences suggest this has not only damaged the relationship with a parent, but it is tiresome and unnecessary. You don't have to forget, but you have every choice as to how you allow your anger to affect those you love. It is no mean feat and this is not written lightly.

Claire despised her Ex's new partner (whom he left her for) showering 'her' children with presents. "I didn't want them coming home with them, the children were so excited with these new gadgets that I couldn't afford, and I remember telling my Ex in front of them to take them back with him. I'll never forget the children's faces; they didn't want to hand them back and wait for another week to play with them. I felt so horrible. I hated myself, but I couldn't help it; I was consumed by jealousy for everything they had that I couldn't buy for them. Working with forgiveness and letting go helped me so much. One day I sat the children down and said I was sorry and that I was happy they had these gifts and how nice it was that Dad's new partner wanted to spoil them. The words felt so hard to say, but afterwards I knew it was like a layer of pain and difficulty that was done and dusted. We never had to have that conversation again; we all just got on with life and I realised that I could be the bigger person in all of this, and it felt good."

Try this: Write down three sentences to use if you find the rage rising and you need to emotionally flatline about your Ex and their new partner for the children's sake:

- "I'm so happy you had a lovely time."
- "How lovely that you had so much fun."
- "It makes me happy knowing you are enjoying yourselves."

Take a deep breath: remember, this work does get easier; you may not think so, but it really does. Your DMMs get used to kinder language and become less demanding.

Remember your children's BS radars – if you need to practise your flatlining face with these or other responses in front of a mirror, then do!

Coping with Family Events

Births, deaths and marriages aren't going anywhere; they may be different, but they're here to stay. Whether you're in a good place or not, some parts of your divorce life will touch and affect not only you, but so many others.

I know someone whose parents cannot stand to be in the same room as each other. They don't speak, they cross over the road to avoid each other, and family events have been tainted by managing the parent who is still stuck in some place that should have been left and emotionally healed many years ago. Weddings, births and family parties have become about managing their unresolved emotional baggage, rather than celebrating the days that were theirs, and are always tainted by the already painful memories of a family that was split so many years ago. Their vitriol and hatred, sadness and grief sadly still exist. It's been there since they were 11 years old and still exists for them, their siblings and their children (the grandchildren) to see and wonder: "Why can't Granny and Grandpa speak to each other?"

A friend, Anne, remembers as a child, teenager and adult, "The whole lot for me was a dreaded and dreadful mess. I remember friends' gatherings and parties well; however, I struggle to recollect the experiences of my own family without flinching, remembering the strained conversations, forced smiles and uncomfortable silences as I unwrapped birthday presents. Or sneaking down to see one parent one weekend and having to lie to the other about where I was, so I didn't feel guilty and could escape their loaded questions. The saving grace and inspiration was the parent who chose to be kind, even though they weren't the one to have an affair and call time on the marriage."

Whether you're both at your child's birthday party, a christening, celebrating a marriage or bidding farewell to a loved one, these are opportunities for you to be a bigger person. You can choose whether you want to ask your children and others to not only manage their own emotions (whether sadness or joy) but also your anger, resentment and dubious behaviour – you really do have the power to do it better, so believe in yourself that you can!

How can you be kind in all of this if your Ex is determined to be otherwise? My answer is this: you just do it anyway. No matter what your Ex is up to, or brings to the table in terms of mood, words or actions, you just get on and be kind. Let your children and others see that you can say hello kindly and with a smile, being warm and friendly. As ever, this is what you have a choice and control over. Let your Ex do what they do; this sadly can only affect their relationship with your children, friends and family. It is gut-wrenching, so sad and wastes precious time, but divorce is a healing journey, of our own wounds and experiences, and is an opportunity to put down the various unhelpful lenses we use to view our adult experiences, which can come from our own childhood.

Layla went to a friend's wedding to which her "cheating b*stard" Ex was also invited. She dressed for herself (not him); she was polite, didn't kick off, and the following day was invited to the post-wedding breakfast of their newly married friends. Her Ex was not invited. It was just her as a thank you and acknowledgement by her friends of what she had the courage to do. She realised then the power of owning her thoughts and her behaviour and how much it had been appreciated.

Try this: Check in with yourself: what can you do to honour who you are during a family event? Maybe spend time getting prepared, have a plan of what you're going to say if you meet each other (and the other partner). Get into your power so if your Ex is unpleasant, you can still access your grace and dignity. After all, their reaction would be about them, not you. Getting comfortable with your preparation toolkit is what you have a choice over.

How to manage family events

You are capable of doing hard things, climbing these divorce mountains and navigating the bumps in the road. Think of a time when you did something hard and you did it well – the sense of achievement and empowerment can be intoxicating, good for building the positive neural pathways and you learn to trust and believe in just how strong you really are! Apply a vision of positive possibilities to family events going forwards so not only you but your children are alright; challenge yourself to begin with the kindness, or get better at it, knowing that every time you do, you empower yourself first and show the children a better and kinder way forward.

How do you do this? It begins before you show up to the event!

Try this: Get all your anger out or manage it better by:

- Setting an Intention for your emotions for the event – write it down and say it as many times as you need to so your DMMs listen!
- Having a therapy session
- Going for a run
- Resisting the temptation to drink alcohol
- Eating something beforehand (avoid the hangry)

- Having a massage or Reiki/energy healing session to help you release some of those emotions in your body (this helps your mind, too)

- Getting some quality sleep banked

- Meditating (see the Divorce Goddess link in the Resources section for some helpful meditations you can try)

- Dressing for you and not your Ex (and definitely not for their new partner) – and don't go having a new hairstyle unless you know it's going to work to boost your confidence!

- Seeing the event as an opportunity rather than a threat – your friends and family will love to see you all brave and courageous

- Create your own mantras and repeat often before you show up!

Mark remembers his 21-year-old daughter's birthday party and his Ex turning up with her new city-living boyfriend who was 'so cool' – the honest (and painful) words of his teenagers. He said he felt like a country bumpkin in comparison until, he said laughing, they all hit the dancefloor. He realised that being 'cool' wasn't all that it was about, and throwing his famous 'dad dance moves' trumped everything as he was joined by all his children on the dancefloor. He said he had to trust that being who he was, was

indeed enough, and the DMMs of comparison needed to go or he
would never have enjoyed his daughter's coming of age.

Here are some mantras to repeat for difficult events:

I can do difficult events.

I love showing up for myself.

I can get through these next few hours.

I am calm, I am wise and I am strong.

I choose to be positive for those I love.

I am in control of my actions.

I am powerful.

I am loved.

Remember, you can't force your Ex to come to the kindness table
at family events. Be you, do your work and know that their stuff
is their stuff, not yours to make good and or figure out. Don't be
giving your lovely energy away by expecting them to do anything
any differently. You can be hopeful and may be surprised!

In the next chapter we will be looking more at moving on from your Ex, giving you tools and practices that are life-changing, so are you ready?

Chapter 6

Onwards and Upwards

This section is to encourage you to stay with the momentum of your phoenix rise, and continue to blossom like a lotus, into all that you are and becoming.

> *I once saw a meme saying, "Stop putting your chairs around someone else's table – remember, you are the table."*

It's time to be your own table – to get wiser, bolder and braver so you can step into your "I am" power by growing your confidence, increasing your self-worth and getting to know yourself better.

Feeling empowered begins by acknowledging all that you're doing in life right now – for example, balancing childcare, coping with lonely nights/weekends, adjusting to changing finances or rampaging hormones, and dealing with a challenging Ex (to list a few) – and knowing all this is enough! But with a commitment to some deep inner work, you'll find your inner magic and strength.

Life has this wonderful way of giving us what we want at the right time. Doing 'the work' attracts the right chairs to your table – when you're kinder to yourself, focus on rebuilding yourself positively and work on letting go of limiting thoughts that stop you getting what you want, life becomes easier. (Limiting thoughts might look like "I'm too old" or "I can't do this" – you get my drift!)

A question I get asked a lot is: "When will I feel different?" I reply, "It could be any time," but it's about doing the work to be your own table – or you could choose to join the divorcees 20 years later who are still angrily putting their chairs around others' tables. It's a kicker, right?! But I promise you, one day you will feel a little different; perhaps you'll notice that the heavy rock that had resided so wretchedly within your belly, for way too long, is no longer there. This doesn't mean all the pain has disappeared; it just means that you, and your life, may be ready to move on. So my advice to you is this: the sooner you look and begin to practise self-kindness or love, by being braver, trusting yourself and the process and doing the work, the sooner you are going to stop lugging that heavy emotional baggage around with you.

This chapter is dedicated to supporting you to get to this place and beyond. I encourage you to take ownership of everything you do mentally, physically, emotionally and spiritually so you can begin rebuilding yourself and walk proudly into the next part of your life. Let's get your 'bucket list' juices flowing (even if you think you don't have anything on that list!) to help you fully reconnect to who you once were so you can blossom into that beautiful lotus flower (that grows out of the stinkiest mud) or rise like a powerful phoenix out of the embers and ashes.

In this chapter, we'll be exploring:

- The opportunities and possibilities that open up when powerful changes happen
- The prospect of a new partner – are you ready, and how do you begin to date again?
- Managing your emotions around your Ex's new partner, as and when the time comes
- Keeping your energy for YOU rather than allowing your thoughts to hang out with your Ex (and maybe their new partner)
- Building your confidence and keeping your spirit strong!
- What your future might look like five or ten years from now... let's get you thinking and begin making it happen!

Opportunities and Possibilities

I love both these words. Without wanting to sound too new-agey, just take a moment to close your eyes and say each one to yourself several times. Feel into the emotions and ideas that come up for you as you say them – I always get goosebumps (or truth bumps)! Do they trigger something in you that makes you want to begin something new, or do you feel the excitement of the unknown? Or do they make you want to cry because they feel so far away at the moment?

Try this: Write down how you feel to be sitting at life's table of opportunities and possibilities.

Your own words may help you see what you want your future to look like. Gift yourself some time to sit with all the possibilities and wild ideas that come to mind. (You could begin with writing down or drawing what the door in front of you looks like – the one that may now be ready for you to walk through!) Bank these positive feelings and use them as healing balm on the tough days.

Give yourself permission to be excited about your future – you might even like to write down a future life Intention. Maybe start with something like this:

I am open to amazing opportunities and possibilities each day and I appreciate and welcome all of them.

In every moment, action and encounter, begin looking for all that is good and out there waiting for you. This may be a smile from a stranger, the sun shining or a win at work. If this feels too much at the moment, that's okay – you may want to come back and reread this chapter when you feel ready. However, from my personal, getting-my-butt-kicked experience, I found that the more I pushed thoughts of the potential of my future to the side, the more work and effort it took to bring this potential into my life. So don't overthink or use 'when I'm ready', as this just gives the DMMs more energy and creates excuses to hold you back.

So, how do you get good at welcoming all this potential into your life when you feel that only the rotten, mudslinging experiences seem to stick? It's time to get present – really present – so that you can begin making more conscious choices that lead to change.

A client, Catherine, got into a pattern of starting her day with thoughts in her head like, "Oh god, I don't want to get up, I don't want to live like this and I'm not strong enough to do this anymore." She realised that she was setting the tone for each day at 5am, consumed with the negative parts of her life and handing away her power with her thoughts – blame, anger, victim! We began working with feel-good habits to start the day so she could silence the DMMs, use the positive thought energy to attract the good stuff each day, and set the tone for the next 12+ hours of her life. Catherine said, "By positively putting it out there that I wanted a good job, the more confident I became to apply for them." She said it was still tough some mornings, but it got easier the more she practised.

If you aren't feeling positive right now, a simple and effective way to reframe your emotions or thoughts is by saying "I'm doing stressed" (so you have more ownership and it feels more temporary), rather than "I'm stressed", which feels more permanent.

To help you get back from a place where you're feeling less than great, not so strong and definitely less positive, try kindly gifting yourself the time to check in with yourself or meditate for a few minutes. (Go to the Divorce Goddess link in the Resources section to access some free meditations.) You stand a greater chance of NOT missing out on what is there for you each day when you take the time to grow your awareness, make time for yourself and build your positive-thinking muscles.

I have clients who say to me, "How can I do this when I'm a single parent just trying to get through the day?" or "My mind is so busy

I can never listen to it" or "How do I do this meditation or being present thing?" But it's not a mysterious, out-of-reach skill – it's simply a case of adopting new daily habits, overriding the DMMs and committing to you. (See the Resources section for a link to my free Taster Mindfulness & Meditation Course.)

Try this: Here are some suggestions to give you time for you each day, or perhaps try one each week to see which works better so the self-care stays:

- Eyes off your devices. Get an app that tells you just how much time you spend down rabbit holes that brings gossip, comparison, judgemental and feel-bad stuff into your life. These 'energy vampires' can make you feel less than you are.

- Don't use your phone as your alarm clock, otherwise you'll be tempted to check messages and emails just before you go to sleep – and then again when you wake up.

- Make the first ten minutes of your day about you. Check in with yourself and ask: "What do I need to do to help myself get through the day? Do I want another day of feeling like sh*t or can I change one small thing?" Commit to opportunities and possibilities by journaling them so you can flip your mindset and create a new, feel-good neural pathway that gives you more capacity to offer kindness to yourself (and help you reduce conflict later).

- With every cup of tea or coffee, or glass of water throughout the day, get into the practice of connecting with your senses: how it feels, tastes and looks as you take the first sip. Being present as you enjoy this drink is a 'now moment', so feel it and have gratitude for it.

- Choose what you're going to wear each day so you wear joy and mischief as you wish (with a nod to the red knickers!) and you leave your house feeling great (or, as a client said to me once, "f*ckable". I have hilarious clients!). Yes, you're going to have days where you turn to track/yoga pants and a sweatshirt. But if you're putting clothes on and thinking "This old stuff, I hate this coat, these jeans make me feel old" – please don't wear them! Wear what brings you joy and puts a smile on your face, and get rid of the stuff that doesn't!

Flipping your thoughts is not only committing to self-kindness but also growing your capacity to better deal with what happens each day. Take JOMO (the glorious Joy of Missing Out) rather than feeling like you're missing out on all the good stuff (FOMO, the crippling Fear of Missing Out). (Chapter 3 looks at FOMO and JOMO in more detail.) It's when you're open to JOMO joy that you encounter more of what you want because you come from a place of acceptance rather than anxiety – and like attracts like! Your kindness gift to yourself each day is that you give yourself time to notice the small things that make you smile and remind you that you're alive, and this forms a more buoyant, emotionally secure and more self-confident you for your future.

If retreating and sinking under the duvet is your go-to today, then know you don't always have to be brave. Know that you always have an opportunity to try again tomorrow, which is another day. Resist sinking into guilt and resist using the word 'should'!

If you know you're consistently starving yourself of possibilities (and remember, the DMMs will tell you it's safer to stay as you are), and you want to live a full and enriched future life moving on, begin embracing all those opportunities and possibilities! Remember, you're here to shine your lovely light and live your best life no matter what has happened! Don't let your Ex be in that part too with unhealed emotions and feelings about them – trust the process.

Rose-Tinted Specs

A word on emotions and feelings about your Ex... and of caution after you've spent time away from each other. Kindness can be emotionally triggering; your heart may surprise you and suddenly get back in the game (or your survival instinct of procreation may kick in) and you may find you want to sleep with your Ex. Some couples end up back in bed (it happens) because they had space to see the better parts of their marriage resurface due to time apart, loneliness and the fear of their divorce reality. This is an opportunity for the DMMs to get busy, asking you whether divorce is a good idea in those quieter moments where you're both getting on well.

Try this: Get yourself a pen and write out your reasons for getting divorced, then read what you've written. Ask yourself, does it feel right? If it feels right, it is right, so listen to your inner voice and reconnect with that good old gut instinct. They'll soon tell you!

It's okay to be confused, divorce brain-fogged and not to trust yourself at times. This is all part of the whole divorce process. However, if you're seriously reconsidering, then please go get your own therapy, couples therapy or help from supportive friends who have seen you both through the hard times. You need to be clear. I am not an advocate of divorce, I just want a kinder process to work for you. It is one of the most difficult decisions to make because you can't see what the future holds, but you always have time so you don't live in regret later. (In my experience, those who leave rarely change their minds. They cannot believe how long it took them to leave when they realised how much better it was on the other side.)

For those who have been left, many have silently or not-so-silently thanked their Exes for leaving once they've turned the corner and, as one client said, "seen the light".

Be mindful that those moments of getting on well can sometimes be a green light for your Ex, with mixed messages and a whole scoopful of false hope. To avoid unrealistic expectations and unclear boundaries (prime ground for confusion, conflict and anger), be clear about why you're being kind (refer to your Divorce Intention), and remind your Ex rather than assuming they remember.

Katie described one afternoon as a car crash waiting to happen. "I had asked for the divorce and wanted it to be as agreeable as possible. We were getting along really well and were actually congratulating ourselves over a bottle of rosé one evening after drop-off as to how well we were doing this separation and divorce thing. Until it came to say goodbye and I sensed that my Ex wanted more, and then he grabbed me and kissed me. I realised then that my own desire for happier co-parenting and peace had been misinterpreted greatly, and he got so angry when I said no. That was a big lesson for us both and took us many steps backwards. My advice is to stay off the alcohol and stay with the Intention, and to remind your Ex of this too!"

Finding a New Partner

Here we'll explore how best to approach finding a future partner, along with the lows and highs that you may or may not be ready for. We'll consider why you're already your own best partner; you just need to remember why.

So… you've stepped back into the dating game! With your life glasses on, with different perspectives and experiences of the people who have impacted, influenced and taught you valuable lessons. Key to finding love again is that you acknowledge, accept and adapt (without selling yourself short) to those you meet moving forwards.

So, no surprise, it takes work to let go of what you think you NEED (big one) and to not go in thinking you're going to be rescued! 'Needing' attracts the wrong energy and person, and you may find yourself back with someone who you thought you'd left… or worse.

The desire to find your final piece of the jigsaw, your forever partner or twin flame, can increase or decrease depending on what you need to work on within yourself. Not wanting to pee on any fireworks, but if you think the end of a bad relationship or marriage is automatically going to send you into the romantic nirvana of new love then you might want to adjust your expectations. That's not to say it doesn't happen, but this 'new partner' stuff happens mostly when we least expect it! I can't tell you how many people I know who have found their big love when they were unprepared, through the most unusual circumstances.

So don't lose hope! Though, if you think meeting someone will complete you, know this. You are already complete, you are whole, you are everything you need and it is all within you. You are your own 'prize', every time.

Dating

Modern-day dating was described to me as walking into the local municipal tip to find love again. Everyone's a little tired, damaged to varying degrees, and desperate to be noticed enough to be taken home and loved!

And dating apps have been described as a narcissist's playground – where you can be anyone you want, treat people badly and there are no repercussions other than being blocked. Eternal optimism and idealism or frustration and anger (or a combination of both) are probably the main attitudes of modern dating that you may find yourself bouncing around between. However, there are many lovely people looking for love.

Dating, as with everything in life, begins with you. You may have an older body, more emotional and mental scars and your DMMs can be unkind and merciless! And the dating world can be brutal, especially if matches are few, a date fails to show, or insidious practices like ghosting (stopping all communication) or breadcrumbing (keeping a non-committal minimal line of chat open) happen. It's easy to get bogged down with "Will I ever meet anyone?" or "What's the matter with me?" You may start criticising yourself and speaking unkindly. Be more mindful and kind to yourself when this happens. Remember, you do not have to be in conflict with yourself! These thoughts are not the truth.

If you think that dating is going to make everything better, it may help you feel less lonely and give you what you need, but you might find the dating experience actually increases feelings of loneliness. Simply focus on yourself first, and look at the reasons why you are out dating (other than to find a wonderful soulmate). Is it because you're lonely, do you feel you need someone to complete you or is this an avoidance tactic regarding other stuff going on in your life? Know you are enough as you are.

Dan remembers "feeling this sense of loneliness many times over, particularly at a weekend, when the children were away and friends busy. I'd settle for a date to fill time – apologies here to those who gave up their time. I'd go home afterwards feeling I had disappointed myself for not being strong enough to have a weekend with me. In all honesty, learning to be with myself and enjoying who I was by being my best friend was the best thing I did for my dating experience."

So yes, go out, join a dating app if this is for you, be discerning, but also enjoy the attention and have fun. There are many lovely people out there that can become friends! Get your laughter muscles working regularly, shine from the inside out and remember – get good at being your own partner first.

Julie, a friend and serial online dater, realised that on dating apps she was being presented with the 'flagstones' of someone, with their basic information, pictures and funny quips designed to hook her. She would then get to work filling in all the cement around each flagstone so they ended up being her perfect man before she had even met them. She was mostly disappointed!

This isn't to say that you shouldn't have high hopes and expectations, but it is really about managing them and asking yourself why you have them.

"Faster in, faster out" – the best words I was ever given for dating!

Remember that you can also be fantastically solo, independent and committed to yourself by doing the personal work to heal those parts that still need work and trust that your future love will find you *because* you did the work. They'll have the same energy and values, and will probably enter your life when you least expect it. Think sliding doors, synchronicity and serendipitous moments.

Thoughts on setting up a dating profile

When you set up your dating profile, ask yourself: does it portray the real you, are you being honest about who you are? Are you putting up old or filtered photos that may cause future internal conflict for you when you're getting ready for a date down the line? Remember to be you, as everyone else is taken.

Ask yourself too, are you even ready to be dating or do you have more emotional clearing work still to do? Whatever the answers, be gentle with yourself, especially after separation and divorce. With confidence at a wobbly low, or dealing with feelings of being discarded, you may be wondering to yourself "Who actually am I?" Also, you might not know what you want, and this is okay; it's normal. Just be aware of how dating makes you feel and how you can reduce your inner conflict with kindness. Think how many other people are dating, slightly confused about who they are and what they want – so get you sorted first!

Going on a date

Congratulations – you're going on a date!

Try this: Get prepared and organised, and if you want to, set yourself an Intention beforehand. Before you step out of the door, consider some of these suggestions from my Instagram followers:

- Get yourself clear on what you want from this date.

- Get yourself clear on what you don't want from this date.

- Always meet somewhere public (never at your home until you know them).

- Consider who pays (I'm generally a splitter).

- Resist drinking on the first date – you don't want to say or do something you may regret!

- If your gut says 'red flag', please listen and don't let the DMMs convince you otherwise.

- Try not to slate your Ex. If you're asked, say something like, "It's work in progress." That way you've covered animosity positively.

- Celebrate your body; love it rather than hating it as you dress for a date. What's the energy you want your date to 'feel' coming off you – confidence or lack of? Dress for you!

- Chat yourself up beforehand with "I love you, I am smart, I am funny, I am gorgeous, I matter". Boost your own confidence, don't rely on booze!

- Are you up for a cheeky snog in the carpark afterwards, or not? Set your boundaries beforehand.

- Just get out there and smile, have fun and see what happens. No longer-term fixed ideas, simply enjoy the time you're out meeting lovely new people also looking for love and friendship.

Have your end-of-the-evening words ready for:

- If you want to see someone again – even if you aren't sure whether they feel the same.
- If you don't want to see someone again – even if they want to.
- A suggestion to check in over the next few days to arrange another date.

If you're feeling anxious after a date, not good enough, unworthy or in any way less than you are, this is your intuition telling you something – please listen! It could be that you aren't ready to date yet, and that's okay. It's highly likely (since you're reading this book) that you're going through big emo stuff, so be kind to yourself and maybe consider taking yourself off dating apps for a while. Every time you listen to your intuition, you are saying YES to yourself.

If it doesn't feel right, it isn't right.

Dating is a balancing act of looking after your own heart while being aware of others'. It's a fine spider's web of emotions: our own, and those also out there searching for love. It is also tempting for many to want rescuing; if this is your modus operandi, you're not going to attract your person. You're more than likely going to attract someone who also wants you for the wrong reasons. You don't have to be rescued – you can do this! Remember, honesty begins with you, so treat yourself well and you'll attract better people in – who treat themselves well, too.

I loved what Debbie, a client, had to say. "Dating after divorce is kind of an opportunistic game available to us as single parents. It was basically me out there again, hopefully not damaging myself further while retaining some degree of grace, positivity and the rosy glow of new romance. It's a different ball game than the one I knew many years ago. It's fun; however, this time we've all got bodies that aren't perfect, but you gotta love yourself and stop trying to be like everyone else!"

Sex

I'm not going to tell you not to jump into bed with anyone, whether after one day of separation or a year. There's no judgement if you desire the skin on skin of being with another, your hormones are rampant and you just want to have sex and lots of it – do what fills you with joy, confidence and helps you back into being you. If you want my permission to jump into bed, have lots of great (or not so great) sex with someone new while enjoying the return of your hormonal and sex-starved inner teenager all over again, you have it! The desire to finally have sex after those perhaps wasteland last years with your Ex can be seductive; to have someone wrap their arms around you and want you is the best feeling. With it comes all those basic fundamental human feelings of connectedness that you may have buried or thought had gone forever. Sex can be a powerful tool to get you back into your empowerment, reconnected to your body and loving yourself again, if you're ready after your separation and divorce.

As with everything, the opposite is also very okay if you're not ready to get stuck in, but instead are waiting for a deeper kind of connection to happen with someone first. There is no race, there's only wasted, regretful time spent by not listening to your intuition more. If it feels too soon, it is too soon. Check in with your body. If you feel like sex isn't for you just yet, you'll know! Enjoy it when you feel the time is right, maybe when you've started loving yourself a bit more first. What you don't want is more conflict in your life, this time with yourself. Note to self though, on that well-used phrase that lurks about in life – if you don't use it, you lose it... I'll leave you to ponder that one, especially if a good friend is saying it's time to get you out there!

Your Ex's New Partner

Is this ever going to be easy? Well, as ever, it depends upon how your relationship ended – whether you were the one who called time on your marriage (or definitely didn't). New partners are going to trigger all sorts of old memories, experiences and insecurities and, as ever, your best tool to support you through this is to be super-gentle with yourself.

Unless your Ex has decided to become a monk or nun, a new partner will present themself at some point. However your marriage ends, there will probably be new partners added into the mix eventually. Call it tough self-love because it can be a painful healing process. Use the following exercise to get yourself used to leaning into the parts that hurt. When we lean in more, we are able to realise that we can be brave and, no, the sabre-toothed tiger hasn't eaten us yet. Leaning into your pain is saying yes to letting go of difficult emotions, instead of sweeping stuff under the carpet that may later come back to bite you.

Try this: This practice helps you look under that carpet, so are you ready?

- Make a cup of tea and find somewhere cosy to sit.
- Get a pen ready to write any notes you may want to make in your journal.

- Set a timer for 5–10 minutes and ensure you won't be disturbed.

- Take several deep and slow breaths into your belly, triggering your body's parasympathetic nervous system – calm stuff.

- Bring to mind your Ex and their new partner (or think of what it would feel like for them to have one) and, while taking several deep breaths, try to see them with your mind's eye. If your partner had an affair and it's still painful, be extra gentle; if it is too hard, exercise self-kindness and come back to your breath.

- Notice how your body is experiencing any thoughts you may have; where do you feel it in your body?

- Take a deep breath into your body, into that part that's holding the emotions – your stomach, shoulders or head, for example. Notice whether your muscles are clenched, or if you feel sick or overwhelmed.

- If it's too much, come out, taking a deep slow breath (try breathing in for a count of seven and out for eleven). If this helps, try it until your thoughts and the DMMs settle.

- Try writing all those feelings down so they're out of your head; envisage how you want to feel about this in the future and see this as part of the process of letting go, getting unhelpful thoughts out of your head and releasing emotions.

- Continue on for as long as you can or want to.

- Thank yourself for this work: it all matters, even though it doesn't feel like it at the time.

(This is also available as a meditation – see the Managing Difficulties meditation at the Divorce Goddess link in the Resources section.)

Never wish your Ex pain, that's not who you are. If your Ex caused you pain, it's because they have pain inside, they need to heal. Wish them healing, that's what they need.

Healing is what we are conditioned to think of as not only painful, but a long and difficult process. The DMMs will try to stop you healing because it takes you to areas of pain that you may not want or be ready to look at just yet, plus the DMMs want to protect you. However, since you have been through so much already, do you not think you owe it to yourself to now gift yourself the opportunity to do this for you and your future? To trust you have your own back and you can be a bigger person through all of this?

Accepting the person your Ex left you for

Each relationship breakup is different. Obviously, I can't see life through your lens of experience, but if your Ex left you for someone else, what I can say is this: if you want life to be easier, set an Intention to be the coolest 'you' moving forwards. When there's nothing for emotional Velcro to stick to, it doesn't stick. The thought of your Ex's new partner might trigger you to be sticky, but resist as often as you can until your neural pathway of intentional coolness is well and truly laid. You don't win any favours (no matter what happened and yes, it is unfair, but this is the reality) by ramping up anger towards your Ex's new partner. You'll be fighting two not one, it will exhaust you and the process of letting go has to start somewhere. Okay, so you may be beyond angry, hurt and wounded, but directing all this towards someone else rather than using this as an opportunity to grow yourself out of the pain pit is what you do have control over. Living in a daily battlefield is exhausting, the kids see and feel it and it serves no one. You may think "but it serves me", which it will in the short term, and you are allowed to be furious, but long term – do you want to be that person still holding all of that anger? Plus, it's much harder to let that long-term hate go – do you want your life to be fuelled by negative thoughts about someone else rather than focusing your energy on you?

Okay, treading lightly here… many times I have heard the words "If it wasn't for her/him…" and I want to ask how good was your relationship at this point that someone was able to come in and mess with it? This doesn't make it okay or right in any way; however, if you're making excuses for your marriage ending by blaming someone else, you may want to ask how happy you both really were, and what were you sweeping under the proverbial marriage carpet that wasn't being addressed?

This can be hard to read, and sometimes the deeper truths hurt. But if an affair happened, it has happened and you can't change that. If you have kids, it's important that you try to heal this pain, anger and emotional trauma, not just for your children's sake, but for your own. Moving forwards dragging this sack of emotions with you is never going to help you.

George remembers buying his wife lovely underwear every birthday and Christmas. He still fancied her but she didn't want sex and she never talked about it. He said he felt rejected and found sex and a relationship elsewhere several times until he found love. His wife knew about the affairs but chose not to talk about them and why they happened. Until he chose to leave for a woman he met and the sh*t hit the fan. He said they never went to counselling and she chose to blame the new partner for everything. He said the whole ending of their marriage was all wrong on so many levels, because neither he nor his wife took any responsibility for at least trying to get their problems sorted. And *now his new partner was blamed and hated and the children were influenced by his ex-wife to hate her too. He knew he did it the wrong way around, he just wished he had had the courage to talk to his wife and walk away without the affairs.*

Self-kindness in all of this is building yourself back up. If you have issues around a new partner who was part of your marriage breakup, then talk to someone (coach/therapist); turn your anger or rage into running or exercising, writing or doing something creative, retraining or starting a new business. Focus on and develop you and grow your resilience – do you first, always.

Anne spent many years at home bringing up the children rather than following her own career. One day her Ex told her he'd met this incredible woman who was everything that she was not, who had a successful career, brought up her children on her own and was brilliant in every way. Anne felt he wanted for her to feel less than she knew deep down that she was. His words hurt. We explored the difficult emotions of anger and resentment around giving up her career to parent her two beloved children. We looked at everything she was as a result. A loving, kind and unselfish mum, who'd given up opportunities in her own life to provide and give lovingly to her children (and her hardworking Ex). This is what she and her Ex had agreed so he could pursue his career. She quietly decided that there was no way she was going to regret her years of being a mum, but would use the energy of her anger and resentment and put it into creating a successful business. That is what she could control, rather than her Ex's deeply painful words.

Be you

There's nothing so powerful as NOT being the person your Ex may have told their new partner about. If your breakup has been full of animosity and anger and you've been made out to be mad, crazy or something else, I invite you now to stop and think of the opportunity that is presented to you instead.

I've always loved the idea of being who my Ex didn't expect me to be.

To not be the person from the relationship ending, but the person you are who is kind, lovely and bigger-hearted than the character your Ex may be trying to project you to be to their new partner to suit their narrative.

Being the bigger person and extending compassion to – wait for it – the double whammy of your Ex and their new partner is immensely satisfying and healing. Think for a minute how good it would feel to be able to drop your children off with your Ex and be able to say hello to each other, to not have to dread the experience and in the process have your children pick up on your energy of negative emotions? Yes, it's going to be difficult, but you're minimising the fallout of something already difficult and painful for yourself and your children. The irony is that when you lean into kindness, it gets less painful even though the need to fight, shout and scream bloody murder at your Ex and the new partner is real and strong.

Think what it would feel like to be invited in for a cup of tea before heading back home and for your children to see that all is well with their parents and their new friends. Isn't this what we teach our children in the playground – to sort out disagreements and find a way to get along instead of increasing division and hate? I appreciate the levels of pain are different, but the lessons in all of this are the same.

You don't have to be the hated and pitied Ex. Stick with your Intention, hold your true North and trust you can be better than the thoughts, words and actions of others. If your children see you being kinder, you're not only teaching them that the good stuff of life can come out of adversity, but your actions and words will stay with them into their older years.

On the other hand, I have spoken to many clients who have expressed not only relief but joy that their Ex had found someone else and was then able to focus on their new partner, taking the heat off their pre- and post-marital dealings. They've actually supported and encouraged their Ex to join a dating site. Clients have also realised that when their Ex's new relationship isn't going well, the heat is turned up on them and once again they become the target of their Ex's dissatisfaction. So if this isn't an invitation to be a kinder human with your Ex's new partner, I don't know what is!

Ultimately, no one wants anyone to be alone, miserable and without love (okay, I know you do sometimes!). If you're struggling with this, ask yourself:

- Is it now time to start letting go and begin to wish my Ex well?
- Can I be grateful for our children and what we had/built/shared together at the time?
- Can I be a bigger person and trust myself to begin responding better and stop reacting?
- Does it serve me each day to hold onto anger in this way?

What to do when your Ex's new partner doesn't like you
Simply, either that's their stuff or what your Ex has told them and they've chosen to believe. What can you do about this? Nothing, except...

Keep showing up as you, be cool and be kind to them, always, no matter how they're acting. Your kids will see it, your Ex will see it and you will be that phoenix rising from the hate ashes.

This isn't doormatting; kindness is clever, especially if you have children together. Keep your focus on your children, keep trusting the process and resist dropping into the new partner's negative energy and triggers.

What if a new partner is actively hostile?

Try this: Remember stepping into kindness is about having boundaries for you first:

- You can choose not to engage if you don't want to. If necessary, have an idea of safe sentences you can use to minimise further conflict. You have a choice every time to do it kindly (in your quieter moments you'll know you were the bigger person) even though it feels hard.

- Don't talk negatively about the new partner in front of your children; this is about you, your Ex and the new partner, not them. If the new partner isn't safe around your children, please seek professional advice around safeguarding (see the Professional Resources part of the Resources section).

- Avoid any extra meetings or ask your Ex to keep communications, pick-ups/drop-offs to just you both for the children's sakes.

- You don't know what the new partner is going through, perhaps with their own Ex, work or children, which may affect how they react to you. None of us ever fully know, so try to bear this in mind; giving someone the benefit of the doubt can be advantageous.

- Accept that this is who they are. It doesn't make it right, but at least you know they are difficult so you have this information to better plan how to manage or cope with meetings, pick-ups/drop-offs or whatever is heading your way.

- If you're worried or anxious, practise deep breathing to calm your DMMs beforehand and any other practice that you know helps you feel less stressed. Do keep a record of their behaviour if you need to.

Forgiveness isn't always easy and sometimes it can feel more painful than what you have already been through. And yet, as the wise writer Marianne Williamson says, "There is no peace without forgiveness."

Staying in Your Own Backyard: Keeping Your Energy for You

I want to share with you a way to flip your thoughts around your Ex, inspired by coach Byron Katie, to help you see how powerful your thoughts can be and how simple it is to take back control of the DMMs when it comes to your Ex.

The backyard concept is designed for you to find and nourish yourself rather than filling your Ex's energy tanks with your lovely energy (as your thoughts, words and actions). It's all about you choosing to find ways to notice where your thoughts are hanging out and guiding them back to focusing on you. You commit to integrating simple, effective and simple (though honestly, not always easy) practices to get you aware of when you're outside your own backyard. You learn to get back into your own space so the difference this beautiful self-kindness practice can make can start to be felt by you and those you love.

Try this: Let's look at how you can get better at not being triggered! Ask yourself:

- What triggers me to think about my Ex (and their new partner)?
- Where does this show up in my body? (Shoulders, head, heart, belly…)

- What can I do to take my DMMs off these thoughts? How can I remind myself? Perhaps writing these strategies down so you are clear, and getting more aware of your bodily sensations may help – and your body will be reminding you anyway!

The resistance to integrating and adopting new practices, routines and thought processes into your life is real. The DMMs want to stay in control, they want to protect you and they want to know what is going on all the time.

We live more now in our heads and have become conditioned to think rather than feel from our hearts. I believe we've also lost much of our ability to sense what feels right for us. There's a tendency to want to find the answers to our dilemmas, pains and emotions outside of us in books, films and by asking others, rather than taking full ownership and trusting our instincts.

For you to get into healing yourself, the first place to look is within you. Kindness for conflict is all about you. You have to put your oxygen mask on first. I want you to reclaim your thoughts, your life and most importantly your energy. Without your energy you have no life, you feel exhausted, depleted, uninspired, at the mercy of whatever is thrown at you by whomever – you become a reactor not a responder, and the neural pathway becomes entrenched so 10 years down the line you are THAT person who is embittered by divorce.

Try this: To get super-clear on why you don't want to be in their backyard:

- I invite you to imagine that each time you think or talk about your Ex or the other person, you are in their 'backyards'. You're putting all your lovely energy into their life, their backyard and their energy field. Where your thoughts go, your energy goes – this is no different!

- How does it feel to be in their backyard? What would it feel like to notice when this is happening and come back to your own backyard? To redirect your energy, your thoughts and actions to nourishing, loving and investing in yourself instead? Do you feel better knowing you have a choice as to whether you spend time in their space or yours?

Keeping your energy in your own backyard is integral to you moving on. Maybe your Ex doesn't know you're talking or thinking about them, but subconsciously their energy field will be picking up on this and keeping you both connected. If you still want to be connected for whatever reason then go ahead and think about them, but if not, it's time to get out of their backyard and back into yours. Get better at noticing this to stop your lovely energy feeding your Ex (and their new partner). If you're still not sure, think about this. Have you ever been talking about someone and then they phoned out of the blue? Or felt your ears burning and you discovered a friend was talking about you? This stuff isn't new, it's been around for aeons, we've just been conditioned and have forgotten about it!

Every time you choose to notice and consciously step back out of your Ex's backyard, it will make it easier for you to do so the next time. And remember, holding resentment in your heart doesn't serve you in any way.

You've Got This! Building Your Confidence

Divorce represents a change in your life, but it also presents an opportunity for you to become smarter, stronger, and a better version of yourself. Commit to positive change and trust in the process. You can grow from this.

Here's the deal: everything you thought you knew about divorce is up for change if you want it to be. How you want to live and what it is you really want; how you want to feel so you can plan your happiest, most confident path through to how to get there is up for grabs. Being out of your comfort zone in your new, not-so-glittery divorced world is the beginning of your amazing life adventure, if you choose to see it this way. This is your journey – it is here for you to take ownership of all of the extraordinary, painful, unexpected, different and uncomfortable zones that make themselves known to you, sometimes many times over, and turn them into something special instead. The DMMs will urge you to run away from going in deeper and try to keep you in the fight club, but it is my hope that you understand by now that the DMMs' path of fight, flight or freeze is where the healing and moving on takes longer and keeps you small.

Try this: Refer to Chapter 2 to find more ways to build your confidence… and here are a few extra for you:

- Begin with doing something differently – walking a different route, wearing a different colour.
- Try a completely new out-of-your-comfort-zone activity like getting yourself into cold water swimming – in the sea or a lake with a group.
- If you can, buy/rent a camper van and get adventuring!
- Learn or train in a skill you've been wanting to try – like forever!
- Plan and plant a vegetable garden (or pots) and grow your own food.

- Write a book, get creative, join a choir, paint!

Do what you love, what feels good rather than what you think is good. Come from the heart and your life will attract more happiness and joy. Build your confidence in the knowledge that you know what is right and works for you.

"One day I woke up," Paola remembers, 'and I felt different and that weightiness that was in my body was no longer there. I knew it hadn't disappeared, but I felt different, like there was less friction and anger, and I felt lighter. I felt ready to move out of my Ex's backyard and start nourishing my own, to focus on me rather than him. This felt so liberating and when I called my long-suffering best friend, she cried. It didn't mean that I wouldn't have my bad days, but I could see light at the end of a long tunnel and I was excited to show my children that their mum could actually do this!"

In that moment of waking up (and it will come) you will be able to smile and say to yourself, "I am back, I have friends and family who love me, my children are okay, I feel freer and I can breathe more easily."

Think of the divorce days as being inside a chrysalis. They are what you need to get through, some days are better and some are bad; however, the butterfly – that is the new you – still has to come out. You may not have choices, you may feel out of control, but the birthing still has to happen. The new you may look different than you thought you would. And until you're ready to embrace rather than resist what has happened, life invariably stays in the cycle of what you don't want rather than what you do.

We know, but may have just temporarily forgotten, with our heads bowed under divorce life, that the sky is always blue above the clouds. As we all step out a little tentatively into the new divorcee world, we have with us our children, a new mix of friends, a smattering of social judgement, less energy and some inner strength telling us we're not done yet!

If you're still wobbling, here's a question. How long, while standing tiptoe on the edge of your new life, do you give yourself before you take the 'OMG' leap of faith? Taking that first step, gaining your independence and flying free are the new joys that come with the post-divorce life that you have in your hands. Remembering who you are, the strong inner you that somehow became a little lost under your relationship, marriage or divorce is worth celebrating, every time.

Add to your bucket list, smile every day, say thank you for everything, good or bad and know it happened to teach you these hard lessons. How you reacted and how you dealt with fear or failure, your strength and undeniable resilience are the lessons you learn for the next part of the journey in your extraordinary life.

Allowing layers of hurt, confusion and fear to fall away gives us a true authentic knowledge of who we are deep down. It can clarify our extraordinary abilities to juggle, to hold it together while being kind, loving and respectful to our own good selves. Loving someone again starts with loving the inner you, who you have always been under life's layers, while trying not to beat yourself up because you failed at a relationship or marriage. Love yourself because you learned some hard lessons and know inside you are still a loving, kind and beautiful soul.

As the wise writer Maya Angelou once wrote: "Success is liking yourself, liking what you do, and liking how you do it."

Your Future

One of my favourite motivational teachers, Wayne Dyer, wrote: "our intention creates our reality". I wrote it down on a sticky note and put it beside my bed as a morning reminder.

Each day you have an opportunity to wake up, to decide how you want your future to be and take a step to get yourself there. You are in control of how you see and what you think about in your life. No matter what's being thrown at you, you have a choice every time as to how you show up, what you say and how you act. No one can take that away from you.

Your resistance will come from the DMMs who want you to stay safe, do what you've always done and get through life. But you haven't gone through everything just to survive moving forwards; you are here to thrive. You are your own barometer as to how your life is in each moment: you are able to navigate the life storms that present themselves and still find inner peace, calm and healing within yourself. All of this has always been there, it is just knowing how, when and where to be able to access it.

Ensure your inner kindness prevails but create your own boundaries with the people you have in your life, with the energy you want to be around. When you do, you say yes to yourself, every time. You have permission to not be selfless, to not beat yourself up when you don't get it right, to make time for yourself to nurture, nourish and love all that is you.

You are the captain of your life ship, you are the kindness within the conflict and you are that beacon of light through your journey to give others permission to do the same.

Get used to being in your power.

A little on the Law of Attraction

I really got into the Law of Attraction – the belief that you attract what you focus on, so having a positive attitude will attract positivity into your life – at the beginning of my own divorce process. When everything felt overwhelming, on the edge of full-blown conflict and facing a financial tsunami, I needed to have faith in something bigger than the daily grind and fight, flight or freeze or, literally, I would have given up. I wanted to believe, and somehow I found that if I kept my thoughts positive and was open to kindness, I attracted kindness and this supported me in taking steps in a positive direction. I chose to believe that at some point opportunities would land… and they did!

I can't tell you how many wonderful things that have happened to me as a result. For example, I was in a relationship that ended (post-divorce) and I needed to move. While unpacking boxes in the new house I found a diary in which I'd written a vision of where I'd wanted to live: "we are living in a smaller house, less rent, an office cabin in the garden, close to the station, friendly neighbourhood"... which was exactly what I moved to!

So try to get better and more aware of where your thoughts go every day, because this, my friends, is where your energy goes. This could look like committing to keeping your thoughts positive (gratitude), your actions in alignment with your beliefs (your Intention) and your health in good stead (more sleep), thus attracting wonderful experiences (lightbulb moments), positive people (new supportive friends) and new opportunities (that job you've always wanted).

Take an example of the opposite, the hallowed ground of many judgements and insecurities – the school playground. It can be a tough place at the best of times, so if you're feeling rotten, angry, confused and sad, your energy is going to reflect this; people pick up on it and they kind of avoid you. This serves to compound how you're feeling. But you're not alone. Think back to a time where you've felt this energy off other people and instinctively avoided them. At the other end of the energy spectrum, consider when someone walks into a room and they have this positive presence. You want to go and hang out with them, and be in their energy. We're far more attracted to someone who is bright, smiley and upfront rather than an angry, low-energy and sad person. What you put out, you get back… do you agree?

This can all feel mightily unfair if you were the one who didn't call time on your relationship, and feel that your partner squashed all the positivity out of you. Yes, you are totally allowed to have bad or low-energy days – this is divorce, after all. But choosing (as early on as you can) to be open to good things happening to you, in amongst all the hard, indescribably awful times, can be the very powerful difference. A morning practice of gratitude helps with this (refer to 'The Power of Gratitude' section in Chapter 4). When you open yourself up to the energy of appreciation, and notice the good, lovely and abundant stuff still in your life, believe me – more comes in!

Attraction is powerful and you have a choice as to how you show up each day. This isn't to say you become a constantly shiny happy person who underneath is exhausted, but you may want to begin by creating a morning check-in practice to help.

Try this: Do a quick morning check-in every day – make it a habit, like brushing your teeth – and ask yourself the following questions:

- How do I feel (sad, lonely, ill, tired, guilty, ashamed, a failure)?
- What do I need (self-love, a hug, a walk with a friend, a therapy or coaching session)?
- What don't I need (to be around people who remind me of my old life, to be locked inside all day without a walk, to have an argument with my Ex, to fall out with a family member)?
- What practices can I use to help myself (meditation, exercise, staying off social media)?

Gift yourself time to wake up earlier so you can check in and write down how you feel, and why. Get your DMM crappy thoughts out early into your notebook or journal and leave them there so they don't stay so much with you throughout the day. As my dad would say, "Start the day as you mean to go on!"

If you're feeling low, you might want to check in more often and notice when the DMMs are plaguing you so you can make adjustments, such as more sleep, exercise, diet or meditation. Reach out to a medical professional, a therapist or coach if it's all becoming too hard and too much.

Think about the Law of Attraction as an opportunity to begin attracting what you want more of in life. Intention is so powerful, and that is what you do have control over.

Try this: Experiment with allowing the Law of Attraction into your life in the following ways:

- Gift yourself time (perhaps when there is no one else around) to think about your future. What would you like to be doing in five or ten years? Are you in a relationship? Running a successful business? In a fulfilling career which brings you the financial freedom to do the things you want to do and experience fully the life you want to live?

- What changes can you make to your physical wellbeing, such as diet, addictive habits or more exercise?

- Who do you see as your friends and who is in your support squad? New single parents? Work colleagues or those you have met from new activities you have taken up?

- Where do you want to be living? How does your home feel for you? Do you have a garden? Access to beautiful outside spaces?
- Do you have a pet, do you want one, and if so, how can you make this happen?

Write down in detail how you can achieve something from this list of ideas. Take your thoughts into the next few years and start seeing possibilities and opportunities!

Try this: I love getting creative and envisioning how I want my life to look like moving forwards. I've been 'manifest boarding' for over ten years now and I'm always blown away by what I put up and what happens as a result – such as working with clients privately on luxe retreats! To create a 'Future of Possibilities and Opportunities Manifest Board':

- Buy yourself a big white board and have some fun sticking photos or pictures on it, drawing or painting your ideas, and getting creative with sticky notes (love them) and positive quotes!
- Create areas such as Health and Happiness, Work and Finance, Future Love, Home, and Family and fill them with wild desires – have some fun with this and be super-imaginative!

- Write yourself a future Intention if this feels the right thing to do for you and put it in the middle of the board.
- Look at it every day and imagine yourself living this life right now!

We can decide to starve ourselves of a beautiful future life that is perhaps based on feelings of not being seen in our last years of marriage and through divorce, so the DMMs scream "Don't put on your brave pants; this will never work!" We become less brave to change what no longer works for us and stay living in fear and anger, becoming hardened and embittered. Erm, that's a NO from me! Or we can take action, empowering ourselves by stepping into that new, exciting wilderness of our future life where we reinvent ourselves, strengthen and grow.

We don't need to know how it is all going to work or happen now. Just by doing this exercise you are putting it all out there – now let life and the 'Universe' help you make it happen!

Divorce is about being given
another goes at living life again.

One part of the whole development process I took a LONG time to get to grips with is what my purpose was in life and where I wanted to see myself in five- or ten-years' time. Over and over again, life would send me serendipitous events, happenings and messages. For example, my Divorce Goddess blog went stellar, and I was on national TV, radio and in the broadsheet newspapers and magazines talking about a kinder way forward during divorce.

Getting an idea of where you are and where you can go is a great way to come back to 'you' to see that you have so much potential when you spend less time thinking about this immediate 'life stuff' and the situations and people that no longer serve you.

I needed to move house for my children to go to a good state school. Renting didn't afford me many options but I kept getting this thought to check a specific home rental site. I took a look and found a perfect house to rent, which was in the school area and also took dogs. I had to laugh! My son had a new friend over and I went outside to tell them the good news – the friend said he lived in that village. I told him what the house looked like and he said it was his house and they were moving and wanted to rent it out! I met the landlord – his dad – at pick-up and happily we got the house. Sometimes you can't make life up!

Be open to change, to not doing it the old way and feeling small and resentful; instead, be open to the new and to being grateful, humble and appreciative.

Focus on the things you feel grateful for now, rather than the things you miss from your married life, by adjusting your mindset. Let go of the victim mindset and you'll naturally attract different things in. They might not be what you originally thought you wanted or needed, but what is right for you at this time.

Sarah said: "I dreaded turning up in a smaller, older car at the school gate, having traded my bigger family car in for financial reasons. I felt I'd be judged and I felt ashamed like I had fallen from grace after divorce. I had spent so long slating my Ex and being angry at us for having to sell our lovely 4x4 that I hated my new car. I had a session with Tosh talking about managing pride and my sense of failure and I realised that the more I was angry about getting out of my smaller car, the worse I felt getting in and driving it. Instead of loving the car and being grateful for having one, I focused on the perceived negative points about it, which kept me in victim 'poor me' mode. It was a powerful mindset change for me, as I no longer felt the need to park at the back of the carpark, I held my head high, parked out front, said hello to everyone and thought "f*ck it". I met humility and it touched me deeply as to how fortunate I really was. I look back now and think, 'OMG, how ungrateful I was for focusing on the negative and less important things in life.'"

Sarah didn't need an expensive car that looked good at the school gates, but one that gave her extra cash in her account at the end of the month!

Sometimes we just have to get out of our own way and to notice when the DMMS are trying to make mountains out of molehills. Sure, not having a swanky car is not great in terms of comfort, sound system, and so on, but notice what it is that triggers you in all of this. Does it matter what anyone thinks? You are no less of a person because your car is smaller or less expensive, right? And if others judge you for this, doesn't it say more about their own fears than it does about who you are as a person? Keep coming back to gratitude for what you do have; build this powerful dopamine muscle rather than letting those DMMs shame you with their unhelpful chatter. Allow yourself to feel good for where you are now and have confidence in where you're going to be in your future.

Remind yourself of your manifest board, and repeat to yourself the words that bolster your feelings of confidence, empowerment and self-worth. These are some of my favourite words that I chant while out walking the dog when I'm feeling wobbly.

I am strong.

I am loved.

I am safe.

I am abundant.

I am healthy.

It is easy to forget on tough days when you haven't slept so well, you feel under attack by your Ex or others, or you feel hormonal or unwell that you are all of the above and more – sometimes you just need to remind yourself. Remember you have your own back first, so be your biggest supporter. And yes, the layers of everyday life, pressures and conditioning can deplete you with the 'you have to be this, think this or act in this way' mindset, and stop you (if you allow them to) from living as your highest, best and loving self.

Moving forwards

Whatever you choose to do moving forwards is ultimately your choice with what you have to work with – whether this is children to care for, money to manifest or your health to nourish, it can feel exciting and overwhelming. So it is good to know that a greater element, often unspoken about, is trusting that there is something bigger than you out there invisibly supporting you in your life, to make whatever happens, happen, so you can live a life filled with joy, happiness and success.

We can open ourselves up to this help by practising acceptance and letting go, often. If you or your actions are blocked and you're trying to control things that aren't working, try pausing and giving the 'something greater than you' time to help you sort it out, make it right or remove it.

Know this too, that you don't always have to get life 'right'; life is about understanding and learning why things happen to us so we can, in our quieter moments, find and understand the lesson, and heal so we can move on.

So, if you find yourself back in your old patterns of sweeping all sorts under the DMM rug and life feels hard, there's more conflict than kindness. Come back to how this feels in your body, check in and gift yourself time to understand why, and make those small adjustments so you can continue with kindness.

The aim is for you to gently release and put down all the emotional baggage so you can live unencumbered, free to love and live with less conflict and with more kindness.

Final Thoughts...

You *will* get through this, despite the many times when the DMMs want you to go into battle rather than offer the hand of kindness to your Ex (and yourself). The more you adopt this kindness through conflict approach, the more you create that all-important neural pathway of a more peaceful, calmer and wiser attitude.

Over the years, people have said to me, "It was easy for you, your Ex was kind," but this came from the place of a hopeful conversation full of opportunities and possibilities around a kinder divorce. To be vulnerable and open to a different way of doing things in divorce (and life) comes from you making that decision, setting that intention to do so and committing fully.

It's easy to go down the well-worn route of anger, fighting back and revenge. That's the old path, the better-known journey, yet the one that leads to future bitterness, less financial freedom and taking everyone that you know and love down that painful track too.

When you decide enough is enough, and choose kindness and compassion over hatred and fear, you show up for those you love – but mostly yourself. As I have said many times in this book, it is about you first, then those you love and finally your Ex.

Your divorce is about you, not your Ex.

You are the person who has to live going forward with the decisions you make and the consequences of your actions and words. Owning them from the beginning of the divorce process, or from wherever you choose to apply kindness for conflict, is what you have a choice over; this is for you, not your Ex, who cannot take ownership of what you say, think or do – only you can do that.

Reconnecting to and believing in yourself is part of the process of divorce. It's an opportunity to empower yourself to believe you are more than something that didn't work (your relationship). You didn't fail, you were just learning all the way through it, and the rest of your beautiful and precious life is still before you with opportunities for you to apply these powerful lessons learned.

Remember…

You are enough.

You matter.

You are worthy.

You are beautiful.

You are kind.

You are strong.

You are perfect in your imperfection.

Small deeds of kindness don't just end because this process has; they are seeded by your own experience, so you too can now be that beacon of light to others and give them permission to know that out of unexpected, difficult and painful endings can come beautiful beginnings.

Resources

Scan the QR code to view all the online resources for this book or visit https://linktr.ee/divorcegoddess

Resources available at the Kindness for Conflict® Divorce Goddess link include:

- Kindness for Conflict Divorce Support Course
- Kindness for Conflict Book Meditations
- Free Taster Mindfulness & Meditation Course
- Freebies – Divorce Goddess Empowerment Library
- How to Stop Thinking About Your Ex Course

- Divorce Goddess Blogs
- *Divorce Goddess* Podcast

The *Divorce Goddess* podcast is available on all major platforms and is a combination of guest interviews and solo podcasts. It is honest, insightful and supports a kinder way through divorce.

For inspiration and support, find the Divorce Goddess on Instagram: @divorcegoddess

***

Professional Resources

Legal

Resolution First for Family Law: resolution.org.uk/find-a-law-professional/ (lawyers, mediators and other professionals)

The Family Law Association – Scotland: familylawassociation.org (lawyers)

The Family Mediation Council: familymediationcouncil.org.uk (mediators)

Financial

Resolution First for Family Law: resolution.org.uk/find-a-law-professional

The Financial Planning Association: financialplanningassociation.org

Therapeutic

British Association for Counselling and Psychotherapy: bacp.co.uk

British Complementary Medicine Association: bcma.co.uk

Children

Children and Family Court Advisory and Support Service (CAFCASS): cafcass.gov.uk

Voices in the Middle: voicesinthemiddle.com

YoungMinds: youngminds.org.uk

Domestic Abuse

My Sisters' House: mysistershouse.info

Surviving Economic Abuse: survivingeconomicabuse.org

The Dash Charity: thedashcharity.org.uk

Financial Advice and Support Charities

Financial Support for Single Parents: singleparents.org.uk/information/benefits/financial-support-for-single-parents

Gingerbread: gingerbread.org.uk

Only Dads: onlydads.org

Only Mums: onlymums.org

Turn2Us: turn2us.org.uk

General

Citizens Advice: citizensadvice.org.uk

Co-Parenting Apps

Cozi: cozi.com

Our Family Wizard: ourfamilywizard.co.uk

We Parent: weparent.app

Self-Development

Shamash Alidina: shamashalidina.com

Brené Brown: brenebrown.com

Jack Canfield: jackcanfield.com

Dr Wayne Dyer: drwaynedyer.com

Pam Grout: pamgrout.com

Wim Hof: wimhofmethod.com

Byron Katie: thework.com

Marie Kondo: konmari.com

Tony Robbins: tonyrobbins.com

Other Mentions in This Book

Maya Angelou: Author of *And Still I Rise*

Kahlil Gibran: Author of *The Prophet* and the poem 'On Children' (https://www.youtube.com/watch?v=z8DSOpsNkt8)

Hafez (poet): poetryfoundation.org/poets/hafez

Susan Jeffers: Author of *Feel the Fear and Do It Anyway* (susanjeffers.com)

Elisabeth Kübler-Ross Foundation: ekrfoundation.org/5-stages-of-grief/5-stages-grief/

Stuff I Love!

Cold water swimming: outdoorswimmingsociety.com

Music – created by Divorce Goddesses!

https://open.spotify.com/playlist/05mu2ykwiQpTSEVyRgRQ02?si=3d9b5db1280f4780

Thanks

Thank you for reading this book to the end. Please buy and gift it, pass it on or recommend it to anyone you know who is thinking about, going through or wanting to reduce conflict in their life and heal through the ending of a relationship or marriage.

My thanks to the kindest mindfulness teacher trainer Shamash Alidina for teaching me the mindfulness tools and practices that brought me back from those dark nights of the soul and gave me the confidence to take this work into the field of divorce.

To Mark Campion for being such an inspiring mentor, and Caroline Cousins for her wonderful therapeutic work on me.

To my very kind, understanding and super-patient editors Kerry Laundon and Rachael Chilvers, who made so much of my mind word-dumping easier to read.

Thanks and appreciation to my mediators Rebecca Hawkins and Claire Webb, you were such an integral part of this process.

To Chrissie Cumming-Walters, Mark Estcourt, Caron Kipping for fact checking, suggestions and supporting!

And to the professionals involved in the divorce arena who are committed to changing the tide, thank you too for your support.

Finally, to all those of you who believe in a kinder, less conflictual and gentler divorce as a pathway through this difficult, painful and challenging life event – there is a better way, one that is available to us all, and it begins with us first.

About Tosh

Tosh Brittan is a divorce coach and therapist, inspirational speaker and thought changer for divorce, supporting women and men to have a calmer, clearer, more confident and emotionally healing experience.

From an international corporate career working with HNWs (High Net Worths), royalty and VIPs to life beyond her own divorce, Tosh combines a professional and discreet divorce coaching service of empowering divorce-changing insights, understanding and empathy with her unique brand of Kindness for Conflict® divorce coaching for people all over the world.

As a qualified mindfulness teacher and Reiki master teacher, Tosh works to support those going through separation and divorce to grow their awareness, manage their emotions and change their mindset, taking them from victim, blame and anger to acceptance, self-kindness and forgiveness so they can move forward confidently and live their best future life.

She has helped many people from all around the world with her coaching, online courses and social media activity. She has also been featured on national TV, radio and newspaper/magazines, not only sharing her story but contributing to campaigns for changes in UK divorce law to support a kinder way through the process.

She started her divorce blog (divorcegoddess.com/blog-page) in 2014, attracting over 100k hits, and in 2019 began the *Divorce Goddess* podcast, which ranked #41 in the US and #16 in the UK Relationship podcast charts after 12 episodes.

She co-authored the #1 bestseller (Personal Health category) *Mindfulness for Challenging Times* with Shamash Alidina and other mindfulness experts, and *Holistic Fashionista Ceremonies: The Art of Ritual Living*. Tosh is a columnist writing about kindness for conflict.

Tosh is a speaker on divorce and mindfulness summits and runs training in companies and for professionals looking to support their employees and clients better through this life experience.

She has a big love for cold sea swimming, and is a mum to two older children. She lives in a market town near the South Downs, Hampshire, in the UK.

Find Tosh on Instagram: @divorcegoddess

Find Tosh on LinkedIn: Tosh Brittan

Printed in Great Britain
by Amazon

19392816R00210